A Special Interest in Computers

Learning and Teaching with Information and Communications Technologies (ICT)

Edited by Paul Brett and Gary Motteram

Published by IATEFL, 3 Kingsdown Chambers,
Kingsdown Park, Whitstable, Kent CT5 2DJ

First published 2000

British Library Cataloguing in Publication Data
Education
Paul Brett and Gary Motteram (Eds.)
  A Special Interest in Computers

ISBN   1 901095 85 1

For a complete list of IATEFL publications, please
write to the above address, or visit the IATEFL web
site at www.iatefl.org

IATEFL Publications Officer: Andy Hopkins. Copy edited by Sue Harmes.
Designed and typeset by White Horse Graphics, Charlbury.
Printed in Britain by Information Press, Eynsham.

CONTENTS

Acknowledgements

We are indebted to the following for permission to reproduce copyright material: Cambridge University Press for an extract from *Cambridge English Course 2* by M Swan and C Walter, CUP (1990), and for an extract from *Dictation* by Paul Davis and Mario Rinvolucri, CUP (1988); *New Scientist* magazine for an extract from *New Scientist* 23 December 1995; *Futuroscope* for the use of photographs from the *Futuroscope* website; Dorling Kindersley for screenshot of *P. B. Bear*; Tim Johns for an extract from his *Remedial Grammar Course*, Birmingham University; Camsoft for screenshot showing use of *Fun with Texts*; Wida Software for screenshot showing use of *Storyboard*; Philips/Nomad and University of Wolverhampton for screenshot from *English for Business*; the British Council Warsaw for materials and screenshots from the British Studies website; Athelstan Publications for an extract from *Teaching Languages with Computers: The State of the Art* by Martha Pennington, Athelstan (1989) and Mark Warschauer and TESOL for an extract from *E-mail for English Teaching: Bringing the Internet and Computer Learning Networks Into the Language Classroom* (1995) by Mark Warschauer (p.8). (Copyright 1995 by Teachers of English to Speakers of Other Languages. All rights reserved. Excerpt used with permission.)

Note

Please ensure that any proposed educational use of a website does not infringe copyright law nor the copyright and use restrictions of the site. In case of doubt, seek permission from the owners of the site.

Introduction

This book is bound together by a number of key ideas, and is aimed at a wide audience, specifically members of IATEFL, but also others who have an interest in finding out what they can do with computers and language learners at the beginning of the 21st century, and more significantly how to do it. As a founder member of the Computer Special Interest Group (SIG) said, 'it is not the technology, it is what you do with it' (Jones, 1986), and it is the 'what you do with it' that we are mostly interested in.

The people from the Computer SIG who produced this book are language teachers or teacher educators like all of the IATEFL membership, but for various reasons we ended up working with technology. We have found it has positive benefits for our learners in all sorts of contexts. Despite not wanting to focus on the technologies as such, we cannot expect to ignore them completely and we have tried to make sure that as many technologies as possible are presented, so that the articles will appeal to as wide an audience as possible. Most of the articles (not surprisingly) mention the World Wide Web, but the uses discussed and the technologies that are mentioned vary considerably. We do make reference to a very wide range of other technologies, for example CD-ROMs, word processors and e-mail.

The book is also about all the SIGs. Each of the chapters has a certain focus in terms of language skill or type of material; some clearly deal with subject material that is from one or another of the SIGs, but all the chapters show material that can be used in a wide range of learning contexts. As many of the SIGs as possible have been referred to: business English, young learners, English for specific purposes, global issues, research and so on. We have tried hard to make sure that there are ideas and materials that can be adapted and used by as many people as possible. The chapters are also built around ideas. By this we mean that each chapter puts the practical parts into a framework of ideas that builds up an effective rationale for doing what is suggested. It is important, in our opinion, that the reasons why we use computers in the ways that we do are effectively explained. Too often books present practical ideas, but with no reference to why they might be useful or effective. This book avoids that trap, but it is still the case that each chapter is written by someone who has practical knowledge of the area they are writing about and the ideas come from their direct experience as teachers.

The computer was the technological innovation of the late 20th century and has made an impact on all our lives, even if we do not actually own one. The computer allows us, amongst other things, to produce high quality written documents, to manage and manipulate numbers, to communicate with each other and to access a bewildering array of information stored on other computers around the globe. These feats are achieved through the use of specific software, word processors, databases, e-mail and browsers for the World Wide Web. All of these have also found their uses in language learning and are featured in the chapters. There is, of course, also software written especially for language learning and these applications are mentioned too. The ideas which form the key part of each of the chapters use a range of the available technology. Some of these technologies are cutting-edge such as digital video in Chapter 3; others are less sophisticated and more commonplace such as databases in Chapter 4, and e-mail in Chapters 1 and 4.

This book has six chapters covering distinct areas. These are: developing writing, using corpora, developing listening, raising cultural awareness, developing speaking and language testing. Each of the six chapters combines three themes in its chosen area. These are considerations of what is thought to be useful and contemporary pedagogic practice based on current literature and research, explanations of specific computer applications or techniques, and practical examples or lesson plans which carry these ideas through to learners.

As has been said, it is with language learning in mind that each of these chapters was written. The study of how second languages are learnt is a relatively recent discipline. These investigations, though, have provided some ideas about the conditions and processes which contribute to language learning and these, in turn, are often the basis of much of our classroom practice. Each of the chapters contains reference to what the author considers to be 'good' classroom practice, and each is suitably referenced to allow the reader more detailed access to the background ideas.

The book starts with a chapter by Diane Slaouti on the role that computers can play in developing writing skills. We have started with this chapter because we feel that many teachers already use word processors and e-mail in their professional life. The move from using it personally, to that of using it publicly with learners, is not as great as in later chapters that involve technologies that readers might be less familiar or comfortable with. Word processors have been used in many language classrooms for some time now, and e-mail has come into its own more recently. The chapter is called *Computers and writing in the second language classroom*. It reflects some of the contexts that Diane has been involved in more recently, such as English with younger learners, as well as examples from other teacher contexts. She suggests many practical ways that the word processor can be exploited to develop our learners' writing skills, and how e-mail and the creation of World Wide Web pages may also be integrated into the development of writing. The lesson ideas focus on an academic perspective with younger learners but can be adapted for any learner group. The topics can be varied to suit learner interests as well as syllabus or curriculum needs.

The chapter by Chris Tribble *Practical uses for language corpora in ELT* provides ideas about how language corpora can be assembled and then used in the classroom in order to raise learners' language awareness. It shows how software that was originally used only for analysing large amounts of mainly written language for research and for dictionary construction, can be used to create classroom corpora for specific groups of learners. It requires, at its most basic, the use of only one computer with a piece of software that fits on a floppy disk. The concordancing software itself, in combination with the Web and CDs, means it is relatively quick and easy for teachers and learners to become language researchers themselves. Teachers can also make use of ready-made commercial corpora, if they do not have time to assemble a corpus themselves. The aims here are to increase understanding of vocabulary, grammar and multi-word units. There are ideas for general English classes, business English and ESP, and of course corpora can be compiled with texts from any subject area. The chapter, like the others, is well referenced so that readers who wish to can go further into the literature on the use of corpora both in and outside the classroom.

The development of listening skills is the main focus of the third chapter, by Paul Brett, *Using computer-based digital video in language learning*. The ideas and information about using video, although they are related here to digital video in a PC environment, also apply to TV-based video. The uses of computer-based digital video, which are exemplified in the lesson ideas in the final section of the chapter, can be applied to many types of learners: young learners, English for specific purposes, or learners of business English. Likewise, by selecting different video clips, the ideas are relevant to the interests of other IATEFL SIGs, for example, global issues or literature and culture. This chapter also shows how technology has changed over time, but that we still need careful pedagogic planning to get the most out of our material. We acknowledge that this paper is at the 'high-tech' end of the computer activities in the book, but change is so fast in the world of computers that it is likely in a few years it will appear very 'low-tech'.

The discussion in ELT about what role culture plays in language learning is a very lively one at the time of writing. The fourth chapter entitled *Building bridges on the Web: using the Internet for cultural studies* by Aidan Thorne and Christine Thorne looks at how the World Wide Web can be used to increase cultural awareness. This chapter focuses on a particular project within one country, Poland, but draws out lessons for anyone thinking of creating web material for their own learners, be it class, school, local area or further afield. Materials here are aimed at a wide age range and cover a number of topics, but could easily be adapted to suit any type of learner in any context.

The fifth chapter, Gary Motteram's *Communicating with computers*, addresses how the computer may be used to develop spoken skills, by making use of simulations, games, databases, or spreadsheets to promote spoken language development through co-operation. It discusses both traditional classrooms and self-access. It also discusses making use of computer-mediated communication to 'talk' to learners all over the world. Increasingly our learners have access to the Internet in schools, at work and at home and are able to extend their experiences of languages in many different ways. The activities here cover a number of topic areas from general to specific language and also deal with a range of software types and technologies. Not all of the activities require high-tech equipment or individual access to computers in order to do the work.

The final chapter by Glenn Fulcher looks at how computers are increasingly being used to help with language testing. It is notable that testing organisations such as TOEFL, UCLES and Pitmans are now using computers to deliver their tests, often alongside more traditional paper-based ones. They are also making use of computers in more traditional ways for marking and statistically analysing the large numbers of ELT exams that they administer. This chapter contains a valuable overview of the state-of-the-art in computer-based testing and shows how computers have been used for testing from the early days of mainframe computers to the present day when tests are conducted on the PC. The article is well referenced and online examples are referred to throughout.

We hope that if you are able to use computers with your learners, these chapters will provide further useful ideas about harnessing their potential in a constructive manner. If you are new to computer-assisted language learning then we hope that the chapters will persuade you that the computer is, in fact, a very powerful tool which can be exploited in a myriad of ways to develop language learning. We also hope you will be stimulated to write about and to share your experiences by publishing them in IATEFL SIG newsletters of all kinds.

Paul Brett and Gary Motteram
February 2000

1 Computers and writing in the second language classroom

Diane Slaouti

Diane Slaouti is Lecturer in Education (TESOL) at the Centre for English Language Studies in Education, University of Manchester, UK, where she is tutor on the Masters courses in educational technology for English language teaching. She is a member of the IATEFL Computer SIG and a committee member of the Media SIG. She has contributed sessions on the use of technology in the classroom and in self-access contexts to various of the SIG workshops over recent years and was a plenary speaker at the Computer SIG/TESOL Spain conference in 1999. She is particularly interested in how teachers can begin to research the impact that different technologies are having on their classroom contexts.   Diane.Slaouti@man.ac.uk

There is perhaps no tool quite so generic as the word processor. It is highly likely that, if teachers have limited experience of using technology, what experience they do have is in order to word process text. Similarly, even if a school has little specific software, where technology is available it is most likely to include a word processor. But this is not the only generic tool that can be used in the teaching of writing. With the advent of wider access to the Internet, writing has moved into domains in which the final product is not necessarily a paper printout but some digital form. Where there is text – in whatever form – writing has been involved. Where do we situate e-mail, for example, in this picture of writing development? What about the World Wide Web which provides a publishing domain for the writer? This chapter will explore some of the approaches to using word processors in the second language writing curriculum and will reflect on the potentials of e-mail and the WWW and their possible roles in relation to the process of writing.

Word processing and writing

What is it that a word processor brings to the writing context? This may seem an obvious question to answer but it is worth reminding ourselves of its characteristics in order to become aware of how best to exploit this tool with language learners.

The word processor by definition 'processes' words or text. It allows us to generate, develop and make multiple modifications to text whilst retaining a tidy look to the page. The computer also allows us to store that text, giving us time to contemplate it, return and review it and make substantial changes should we wish to without involving lengthy rewriting. This ease with which improvements can be made to a text, whether they be revisions or additions, encourages drafting and redrafting, an essential element of the writing process (Daiute, 1985; Phinney, 1989; Neu and Scarcella, 1991; Hyland, 1993).

The word processor offers the same potential to our learners and as a tool they are likely to encounter in their daily lives, this in itself would seem an appropriate justification for its use. Any tool which facilitates writing in a foreign language must also be worth considering. The language learner prone to making errors as language is developing takes encouragement from the fact that error is not permanent. Once edited, mistakes disappear forever. The teacher's written feedback on a text, equally, need not remain forever as a mark on the page. Text can be corrected, reworked, saved and printed with a permanent record of progress as that feedback is acted upon.

The word processor would appear to allow a writer the easiest route to enabling the writing process to arrive at the best product possible, although admittedly many writers do not use this particular tool! Some research suggests that writing tools are very much related to more individual composing behaviours (Chandler, 1993) and as such the word processor may not be the natural tool for all writers.

The potential is, nevertheless, evident. But is this potential immediately accessible to all learners? Is it simply a matter of providing the computers and software? How also might the added 'language development factor' impact on how the language teacher exploits the tool?

This chapter addresses the following areas:

– the relationship between 'computer' skills and language development
– the importance of task in the bid to encourage improved writing
– effective integration of word processing into the teaching context

'Computer' skills or language skills?

Various studies (Piper, 1987; Phinney, 1989; Neu and Scarcella, 1991; Hyland, 1993) discuss how being offered the opportunity to exploit the word processor influences learner attitudes to writing and these are reported as being largely positive. Observations related to learner attitude relate to willingness to spend more time composing, greater attention to the task in hand, willingness to see the writing as a fluid piece of work, 'under development' (Phinney,1989: 87).

Different writers have, however, recognised that their findings may have been influenced by the fact that their learners have had varying degrees of familiarity with the computer. Neu and Scarcella (1991: 174–185) acknowledge this fact in their study which concentrated on learner attitudes.

> an initial positive attitude toward writing on the computer could not be expected to persist if students found that learning and using the computer proved to be difficult or anxiety-producing.

In whatever learning context we consider, anxiety will impinge on learning effectiveness and it is evident that some learners do feel insecure with the technology, although it is fair to say that the situation today is already vastly different from that of just a few years ago.

Nevertheless, the way in which we develop the appropriate skills with which learners might make effective use of this tool deserves reflection. Being able to provide learners with a keyboard familiarisation course beyond the language classroom may be a luxury we are often unable to provide, although some writers report on how they have developed such courses (Hyland, 1993; Lam and Pennington, 1995). Perhaps an alternative solution is to consider how we might use the word processor to facilitate a number of language tasks whilst developing the very familiarity our learners need.

First of all, in order to make the most of this tool, which are the key functions that it would be useful to ensure learners can use? Look at the following script written by an L2 learner with its annotations indicating possible revisions. Which features of the word processor would facilitate the suggested revisions?

Well done so far.

Don't forget to spellcheck your work.

Penguin Island and Maliba are in the Pacific. Penguin Island is 15km from Maliba. There is some simlilarities between them but they are also very different. — Grammar?

Penguin Island and Maliba are approximately the same size. Penguin Island is rectangular in shape and has a rocky coastline. Maliba is oval in shape and has beeaches on the east coast. Penguin Island is an agricultural community.

Can you try to link these sentences?

The people on Penguin Island make a living from sheep farming and fishing. The people on Maliba make a living from tourism. They have built hotels and golf courses for the tourists. The airport also helps to bring tourists to the island.

Penguin Island only has one fishing village on the northeast coast. Maliba has villages around the island. The village on Penguin Island is linked to a monastery by a footpath. The villages on Maliba are linked by main roads. There is also an airport on Maliba.

Think about how we use articles. Which of these ideas would come first?

This sentence really introduces the ideas in the paragraph before. Try moving it there.

Maliba is more densely populated than Penguin Island and transport and communications are much better.

To improve this piece of writing, the writer needs to:

– insert the cursor at a particular point on the screen and type small amounts of text
– delete existing text and retype
– move a block of text from one position to another
– spell-check the text, although in the word processor that I am using to write this (*Word 97*), misspellings are underlined as I write. This may be a potentially positive feature, though a large amount of 'red underlinings' is frustrating and can accentuate a preoccupation with accuracy on screen. It may be worth considering disabling this function in some contexts.

To achieve the above, a user needs to at least know the basic features of the tool: where to locate certain keys on the keyboard and certain functions on a toolbar as well as how to manipulate a mouse. If learners need time to become familiar with those functions, then this is an additional burden to that of thinking about language, and especially so if they are required to produce a free piece of writing. The user will need some knowledge of file management as any computer-based task will also involve saving a text as a file to a directory or to a disk, and drafting and revising possibilities also involve retrieving that file at a later date.

But there is another way of looking at the relationship between features of the word processor and writing. Working with texts in this way is not new to the language classroom. Open any textbook and you see the following task types: gap-fills involving the *insertion* of words, editing tasks involving the *deletion* or *insertion* of words, matching tasks or jigsaw tasks involving the *moving around* of words or paragraphs. In most classrooms learners complete these tasks, correct them and probably stop there. If they are not quite right, they rarely *edit* them on paper to take away a perfect model. Many teachers would suggest that time is a major constraint in working towards a learner-produced 'good copy' quite apart from the learners objecting to such 'redrafting' of tasks. However, perhaps the word processor might have a role to play in such language tasks.

Here is a preliminary example of a task that takes advantage of the features of the word processor. Read the task instructions and think about the computer skills needed to accomplish this, the learning focus of the task and how the task setting influences learner interaction.

REPAIRING THE TEXT

This text is not quite complete: all the verbs have disappeared. Work with a partner to repair the text before looking at a model. Practise using the mouse to position the cursor before typing.

These friends of mine a new carpet, so they to the shop and one and the carpet-fitter round to fit it while they out at work. When he, he that there a bump right in the middle. He that this be a pack of cigarettes that he absent-mindedly, so he up and down on the bump until it flat. The family home and the carpet. Then they the man if he their pet canary which missing. It then that he his cigarettes on the hall table!

In terms of *computer skills*, the learners need to be able to position the cursor at a chosen point, type in a word, perhaps use the space bar to separate words in the text and to use the delete key if they make an error.

In terms of *language focus,* they are reading for meaning, generating appropriate lexis and focusing on appropriate grammatical construction.

Finally, in terms of *classroom interaction*, they are collaborating with a partner, generating language around the task. Even monolingual classes with all the risks of not negotiating in L2 still generate English because they are talking *about* language.

This could be done on paper. But that would involve writing the text out and, if the learners change their mind or make mistakes as they go along, this can result in a very messy piece of work. There are similar textbook tasks that are also facilitated by use of the word processor. Here is one from the *Cambridge English Course 2* (Swan and Walter, 1990).

HOW PEOPLE LIVE
Highlight each piece of information and copy and paste to create two texts, one about Australian Aborigines, the other about Amazonian Indians.

The Karadjere people live in the desert of Western Australia,	The Amazonian Indians live in the Amazon Basin in Brazil,

where the climate is very hot.
where the climate is hot and wet:
and the rest of the year is dry.
It rains from January to March,
It rains for nine to ten months of the year.

They travel by canoe.
They do not live in one place,
They live in villages;
but travel around on foot.
They sleep in shelters made of dry tree branches.
and the roofs are made of palm leaves.
their houses are made of wood,
Several families live in each house.
Their food is fruit, nuts and kangaroo meat,
They eat fruit and vegetables, fish and meat from animals and birds
and they eat fish in the wet season;
(for example monkeys, wild pigs, parrots).
They also make bread from grass seeds.
The Karadjere like music, dancing and telling stories.
Water is often difficult to find.
They do not wear many clothes.
They do not wear many clothes.

Many teachers handle this type of task in the classroom by providing the cut-up text as a jigsaw activity. *Physically* handling text like this generates meaningful collaboration around texts with learners. So why move it into the word processor? The most obvious reason is perhaps the facility with which learners can create their own final text and print it off. However, more than that, such tasks within the word-processing environment are in their own right developing very real skills that will later be transferred to more extended writing tasks. These are, moreover, not simply the physical skills of knowing how to achieve the series of moves which consist of highlighting, copying and pasting text but also the associated metacognitive skills of relating word-processing functions to text development in its own right.

We are, therefore, doing two things with such tasks: clearly associating the *tool* with the *process* of generating a written text and taking advantage of the features of the tool to facilitate a repertoire of language learning tasks that are familiar to us.

A further key point in relation to the tool itself and the very task of writing is the public nature of the computer screen. This brings with it several important issues. Firstly, the fact that text revisions can be dynamically demonstrated by the teacher or by another learner. Consider, for example, the need to separate the text in our sample into two paragraphs. In a hand-written piece, the best we can do is indicate a paragraph break, but the full significance of this is not visible to the learner. Paragraphing is accompanied by the notion of 'white space' separating one paragraph from another. Piper (1987: 121) describes how the demonstration of this to one of her learners was immediately revelatory. On inserting the cursor at the appropriate point and pressing the enter key a new paragraph appears before the learners' eyes. The physical space created is a visual representation of the concept of paragraph. The ability to demonstrate other text modifications such as reorganising by using block and move facilities is equally powerful. The screen area is, thus, shared by the writer(s) and the teacher. It becomes a ground not only for suggestion but also for immediate demonstration in a way that paper has never allowed us to achieve.

Towards developing writing skills

The potential of the word processor to ease the writing process cannot, therefore, be disputed. The writing of this book would be much more difficult, if it were not for the ease with which text can be written, contemplated, revised. If we consider the sample writing with its annotations seen previously, making those changes without the use of the word processor would have probably seemed an onerous task to the learner and one which, because of the time it requires to rewrite, a teacher might not always insist on. This potential for facilitating revision brings a further benefit. Writers report that the use of word processors encourages 'experimentation and risk-taking' (Cochran-Smith, 1991: 134). We might, therefore, presume that because nothing is written in stone, then learners will produce more text of increasing quality. But this will not come immediately. The initial familiarisation period we have already suggested is vital in both enabling learners to know the potential of the tool they are using and in reassuring them that they are in control of the text before them.

Findings of studies into word processing and writing quality are, in fact, rather confusing. Hyland (1993: 22) highlights the fact that findings are diverse because the variables of each context are in themselves so diverse. Factors such as learner attitude to writing, teacher attitude to computers, word processing familiarity, individual writing ability, time allocated to use of computers, integration into the syllabus, have all been seen to vary in the different studies. Some studies do, however, begin to draw more positive conclusions. Neu and Scarcella (1991: 170) report learners feeling that:

> word processing benefited their performance in writing. They also felt that using word processing helped concentrate their attention on certain aspects of their writing (e.g. grammar, word choice, organisation and transitions).

Bangert-Drowns (1993: 87–88), reviewing related literature, interestingly found that:

> basic writers tend to benefit more from word processing than higher ability students; … that the word processing experience has a motivational impact on basic writers, encouraging all to engage in writing tasks more wholeheartedly.

This latter claim is reassuring if we consider when to give learners access to the word processor as a language learning tool. There is sometimes some reticence in doing so in the early stages of language learning in the belief that learners' concerns with language issues will result in little text production and, therefore, little reason to use the word processor.

And it is clear that often little is produced – especially in the early stages of free writing. But this issue of whether we bother with using the word processor when so little 'writing' would appear to, on occasions, result on screen is of relevance to the issue of developing quality in writing. If learners are not given the opportunity to use the tool effectively, then it is hardly surprising that they become blocked at the earlier stages. Pennington (1996) offers a useful discussion of the stages through which the L2 'computer writer' must pass. These are:

- writing easier
- writing more
- writing differently
- writing better

Perhaps these stages do not appear to be particularly specific to the 'computer writer' context. In any writing context, as learners write more easily, they tend to write more, at which stage they can begin to make use of the recursive cycle associated with process writing which subsequently produces better writing. Pennington, however, analyses these stages specifically in terms of what the word processor brings to each. The higher order stages of 'writing better' will result in the word processor coming into its own. Drafting and redrafting events will only be possible once more text begins to be produced and once language begins to be generated with more confidence. But learners must be given the opportunity to produce that text.

Integrating word processing

All of which brings us to the issue of providing opportunities for learners to exploit word processing. These opportunities may involve considering how we approach writing in the second language classroom and subsequently allowing the word processor to play an integrative role in the process of developing text. It may equally involve finding opportunities where the word processor might aid the teacher in creating more effective tasks. One effective starting point has already emerged: the textbook tasks which provide opportunities not simply 'to use the word processor' but to create meaningful writing opportunities where perhaps the original focus of the textbook is not to do so.

The tasks that we have seen so far, whilst providing a more controlled writing environment, do result in learners possessing a complete text even in the early stages when the problem of 'amount of text' is of concern. Such control can be relinquished, either partially or totally, as language and skills develop. A combination of control and freer writing often proves a successful transition. Tasks which require some 'working of a given text' in the early stages leading to learners providing their own text to finish off, once again ensures a notion of completeness. One successful activity which moves between structured and freer writing is the guided dictation. I owe this example to Paul Davis and Mario Rinvolucri (from *Dictation* Cambridge University Press, 1988).

GUIDED DICTATION

Learners open up a new word processing document, type in their names at the top, then save. The task moves between dictation and freer writing. At each stage the learners are instructed to type as quickly as possible and to be mainly concerned with committing ideas to screen.

Dictation
Giovanni was having a bad day at school. His history teacher wasn't happy with him.

Creative writing
Now work together to write the dialogue between Giovanni and his teacher.

Dictation
At the end of the school day, he went home feeling miserable. He went straight into the kitchen where his mum was making the dinner.

Creative writing
Now work together to describe Giovanni's mum.

Dictation
Eventually Giovanni's mum called the family to the table. They all sat down but it didn't take long for Giovanni's mum and dad to start arguing.

Creative writing
Work together to write the conversation between Giovanni's mum and dad.

Dictation
Giovanni couldn't stand it any longer. He pushed back his chair and stormed out of the room, banging the door behind him.

Creative writing
Now complete your story.

A task such as this brings various benefits. First of all it moves the writing along, discouraging learners from deliberating too much over every word of every sentence. It is important to try this task with time constraints set at each stage. This approximates to the technique of quickwriting or nutshelling (Jacobs, 1986) which encourages the *generation of ideas*. Quickwriting does produce numerous errors since the learners are focused on content, not accuracy. Using a spellchecker following this stage, however, can generate a lot of meaningful text-based discussion in its own right. However, as I have mentioned previously, the underlining feature which shows incorrect spelling (at least against the internal dictionary of your word processor) is an alternative and immediate visual prompt. Whatever tool is used, learners engage in a second level of 'talking about text' to decide what their intended text should be.

The task also provides the teacher with a view on particular areas for development. Input can be provided in any of the key areas of the text: description, dialogue, narrative, after which learners can then return to embellish their growing text.

As with any writing task, the subject of the text is open to the teacher to determine in relation to the learners and their language skills and in relation to their experience of the world. It is the very fact that the task is accomplished within the word-processing environment, however, that allows the *writing process* to be fully activated.

Once learners begin to generate more extended text, the full potential of the word-processing environment can be unleashed – in theory. I have witnessed on many occasions the tool being used to produce a good-looking copy of text but not really being used to help learners develop text. I worked recently with teachers using word processing for the first time with 14-year-old bilingual learners. They had noticed how the children wrote on paper, transferred their text on to the screen and then seemed content at the printed output. We discussed why this had happened and concluded that perhaps the task itself had not encouraged an approach that developed the children's awareness of the process of writing in its own right.

The following sequence of integrated activities has been reproduced in some detail to show how it is the task that will unleash the full potential of the word processor and its intrinsic relation to process writing. The resources mentioned in this example were collected whilst working with second language learners in the UK. These learners were following English for Academic Purposes courses preparing them for study at undergraduate and postgraduate level in UK universities. Similar resources can be gathered from various text and broadcast sources to create a similar sequence of activities.

The lesson moves through a number of stages towards writing in editing teams:

1. reading a short report from the *New Scientist* (a popular science magazine) to confirm the notion of genre-specific content
2. video viewing of a short report from a popular science and technology programme
3. producing a written version of the broadcast report
4. producing a number of short entries for a magazine explaining about new developments for a non-expert audience

Stage one: Reading

Pre-reading task

Students predict what sort of information they would expect to hear/see if they watch or read a report about a new invention or development.

This should result in:

- What is it called?
- What does it do?
- What does it consist of?
- How does it work?
- Any problems/need for future development or testing?

Reading task

Students read this extract from the *New Scientist* reporting on a new computer development and take notes using the questions they have predicted during the pre-reading task.

DETECTING THE REAL THING

Most noses are not educated enough to tell whether the whisky we are drinking is a genuine blend or a fake. To combat the rise in fake products, The Scotch Whisky Research Institute – funded by the 12 largest whisky companies in Scotland – has developed a computer-based "Whisky Taster", capable of distinguishing between a genuine scotch whisky and a fake one.

There are nearly 100 malt whiskies and each blend is created by mixing 30 or 40 of them together. By analysing data from ten years of whisky production, scientists separated the different compounds, or congeners, which make up the five main volatile flavours. The combination of such compounds in each blend is the signature to their authenticity. Scientists subsequently developed the Whisky Taster itself, which, in fact, consists of a PC-based neural network. This was then "trained" to analyse the compounds within each blend, thus identifying any which do not match genuine combinations.

New Scientist 2009, 23 December 1995

Stage two: Video viewing

Students now watch a short report (about 3–4 minutes) from a popular BBC science and technology programme: *Tomorrow's World*. They apply the same questions to the report. The report used in this lesson was of a fire-resistant fabric developed to protect houses at threat from bush fires in Australia. The fabric was intended to literally envelope the whole structure like a huge insulating blanket.

Stage three: Summary writing

Students now produce a word-processed summary of the information they have noted using the organisational model they developed from the reading task.

When they have finished, they exchange texts with a partner and comment on each other's work, helping each other to improve the accuracy of the text. If they feel information is missing or misplaced, they make suggestions.

Stage four: Selective video viewing

Students compile a magazine section or a poster display on various recent developments in science and technology. These should be written for the non-expert audience, interested in science and technology. In pairs, they select one of the following video reports according to interest and find out the information they need to write their report:

– The Green Camera (detecting cars with faulty exhaust systems)
– Virtual Surgery (using virtual reality to train doctors)
– The Flying Doctors (mass vaccination using mosquitoes)
– Forensic footprinting (using forensic science to catch burglars)
– Frogmatting (a new invention to soak up oil from spills without the use of chemicals)
– Clear water (natural water purification for the developing world)

Stage five: Editing

Once students have completed their texts, they form an editing team. They read each other's reports and use the following checklist:

– Do any of you include information that is missing from others?
– Would you like those reports to contain any more detail?
– If necessary, review your video extract and revise your reports.
– Decide on the layout of your poster. Do you want any graphical information?
– Put the reports together into one document.

By the final stages, the learners are producing their own extended texts and the sequence of tasks supports the process. This lesson allows writers' choice but does not neglect the need to become familiar with the genre of the text expected. It also gives explicit reminders of the role a peer reader can play and via the instructions, encourages learners to return to their word-processed text and to review and redraft. The use of the word processor to accomplish the task means that learners can both understand the recursive nature of writing and make significant moves to develop their drafts.

Similar lessons can be crafted out of an assembly of different resources, or learners working together on a project can choose to investigate what they wish within the parameters of the target writing output. Producing a tourist brochure by assembling information about different places to visit in a town is a familiar example. Information about places to visit typically includes opening times, entry fee, key points of interest. Again, tourist brochures may have genre-specific features that require examination before the learners embark on their texts.

WHAT TO DO AT FUTUROSCOPE !

Futuroscope isn't just a fun theme Park but also an educational experience.

Students will be able to experience how rides work and how they are made. They can attend conferences where they will explain this. Students will be able to have a good time aswell as learning side of things A lecture will also be held to show the students how all the cinemas work including the '360' cinema, showing the photographic side. The students can also attend a theme Park within Futuroscope where there are special rollercoaster rides. There is plenty for everyone to look forward to -even adults.

There are plenty of fun things the students can do!

Students can participate in the showing of various films in our brand new 360 cinema. You can visit the magic Tapis, where it is a series of elevators going up towards the sky at different heights and angles. The students will also be able to visit the Aquascope - an indoor water world Ther are plenty more things for the students to enjoy.

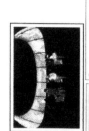

FACILITIES

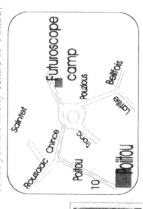

These are just two types of Facilities that are available at Futuroscope. It can be anything from a crystal Restaurant to an elevated Hotel. There is a wide range of different qualities,from 1* to 5*. The hotels are no more than a 30 minute walk from Futuroscope. All the restaurant have a variety of menus. There is also a variety of transport to help you to get around.

MAP FOR FUTUROSCOPE
(once you are in city centre of Poitou)

Scintet
Rousaac
Chince
Poitou
Tron
Lafille
Bellfois
Pouzious
Futuroscope camp
Poitou
10

Word processor as desktop publisher

This notion of learners as publishers is further facilitated by today's writing tools. If we consider the suggestion of working on tourist brochures as a genre in its own right, this is characterised by selecting graphic as well as textual information. The ease with which pictures can now be imported into the word-processed document adds to the near real-world quality with which such documents can now be produced. Learners can also make choices about design of a text in terms of layout and choice of fonts and are able to easily achieve the impact they want. This view of word processor as desktop publisher allows learners to see a piece of writing as a synthesis of the words themselves and other supporting features, all of which go to making up the final document. Working towards such publication provides for effective collaborative activity in the classroom. The production of text is, moreover, one element of a series of integrated stages that include research, selection and processing of information (both written and visual), negotiation about appropriate tools and design.

Learners might also be encouraged in a simulation of a larger project to do more than simply planning and producing one text. This can also be done at differing levels of writing and language experience and with different ages of learners. Here is an example carried out with a group of teenage learners. Their task was to design a number of texts that would be needed for a school trip. The class group decided what would be needed and this resulted in the following items:

- a letter giving basic information about the trip (place, dates, costs, accommodation if the trip required this) and asking for an indication of interest
- a letter to acknowledge interest and to inform participants about arrangements for the trip (payment, travel arrangements, meeting time and place)
- a leaflet about the place to be visited

On the page opposite is the leaflet designed by one of the groups for the French theme park, *Futuroscope*. The information and graphic support was found at the *Futuroscope* website.

It is clear that each document will require various levels of decision making. Teacher and learners may need to look at sample texts from the point of view of determining genre-specific features and necessary language. The sequence of tasks will certainly involve researching information from different sources, planning, organising and designing, drafting, redrafting, editing.

The topic of such simulated writing projects can be varied; the location does not have to be local. The WWW can now provide learners with information about places they have visited across the other side of the world, as was the case in this example. CD-ROMs are an equally immediate resource.

In fact, this facility to use digital resources within word-processing packages is just one of the more recent features of word-processing packages. Another is the potential to create interactive tasks that support writing. Features such as the ability to create drop-down fields enabling learners to make choices on screen can provide more guided writing support.

The picture source on the next page is the young learners CD-ROM *P.B.Bear* by Dorling Kindersley. In-built to the CD is the facility to copy the screens and paste them into the word processor, a feature in many reference CD-ROMs too. The drop-down fields presenting

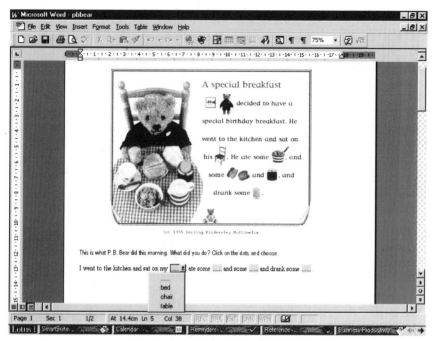

P. B. Bear – Copyright Dorling Kindersley by kind permission

lexical choices to the learners are created using the form field function in the word processor. Protecting the document (a function of a word processor) allows learners to do this task on screen, making the choice they want for their own piece of writing and printing it off. Support can gradually be relinquished or other types of choice can be given. Learners might subsequently copy their own pictures or screens to illustrate their own work.

From paper to digital output

We have so far considered publication in terms of paper-based output. It is true that, until recent years, the word processor has been associated with printed publication. This, however, is quickly changing with the rapid expansion of access within educational institutions to the Internet and with it versions of word processors that allow publication immediately in a digital form. A word-processed document can, at the click of a button, be transformed into an HTML (hypertext mark-up language) text capable of being displayed in a web browser either locally on an institutional Intranet or to the outside world.

Text is, furthermore, not simply created within a word processor but also within communications tools such as e-mail. It is clear, however, that although e-mail is a text-based environment, it is associated with computer-mediated communication. The text that results within this environment often resembles speaking as much as it does writing. Does it, therefore, deserve attention in a chapter about writing tools? If so, what is the relation between this and the World Wide Web and the writing process?

The thrust of the argument in this chapter so far has been that word processors facilitate the generation and revision of text. In the tasks demonstrated, however, a clear emphasis has been on sharing texts around the computer screen. This sharing of text may happen around one screen; it may also happen within a networked environment in which the potential to share and collaborate can take place both within and beyond the classroom walls. In such an environment, learners are able to both communicate their ideas to one another and collaborate on writing outcomes. Various projects have been reported in the second language learning literature e.g. Beauvois, 1997; Warschauer, 1997; Sullivan & Pratt, 1996; Warschauer et al, 1996. One tool that has particularly facilitated communication of ideas has been e-mail. In the final part of this chapter, I would like to share a project undertaken recently with a group of learners in a secondary context, a project in which the role of e-mail in relation to developing writing skills was subjected to some scrutiny.

E-mail can provide communication between members of a learning group. In many contexts the use of e-mail is, in fact, largely characterised by the 'keypal' idea, which means using e-mail to put learners in contact with peers from other cultures. The potential of the 'global classroom' (Soh & Soon, 1991) is enticing. In such communication it is probably no surprise that e-mail facilitates the pre-writing stage, that is, the informing and generation of ideas. (See chapters by Motteram and Thorne & Thorne in this volume for further discussion on the topic of e-mail.)

However, this is perhaps only one dimension of the contribution e-mail might make to the writing process. Kroonenberg (1995: 29), who reports on the relation between e-mail activity and oral work, makes an interesting claim for the tool:

> Thoughts and arguments first composed in writing on email give students reflection time prior to engaging in oral work… the quality of the argument is enhanced and thinking is more creative than without this kind of preparation.

In a research project that I have been involved in with local teachers in schools with large numbers of EAL (English as an Additional Language) children, there has been evidence of a similar claim to be made for e-mail and writing.

In its initial phase (Slaouti, 1998), the project involved a group of bilingual learners in a local secondary school being linked up with a teacher partner from the Centre for English Language Studies in Education at the University of Manchester. The learners communicated with their partners over a period of eight months, towards the end of which they created a personal web page with the writing that had been part of the e-mail exchanges. The content of the e-mail messages obviously revolved around partners getting to know each other, exchanging 'autobiographical' information. During the period of communication, we logged all the communications and looked at the relationship between e-mail messages and the final pieces of writing.

There were some key observations of relevance to the e-mail/writing debate, the first of these being how communication was maintained throughout the period and the relationship between communications and task.

The diagram on the next page illustrates a typical pattern of communication evident for most of the teacher–learner pairs.

Ahmed: Somali pupil, Year 10

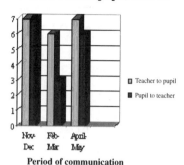

Period of communication

Oumar: Urdu, Year 8

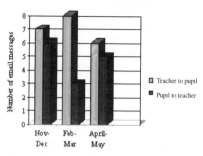

Period of communication

The communications that flowed in the early months were driven by the getting-to-know you manoeuvres on either side. The dip evident in the middle period could be explained by various factors including technological difficulties and a period of lull as the 'keypal' idea began perhaps to wane slightly. The rise in the latter period coincides with the writing task being driven towards the children publishing their autobiographies on their web page.

If we then look at the content of the messages over these periods, again some interesting observations begin to emerge. The e-mail texts contained language errors and this remained so throughout the project for most of the learners as long as they were writing in the e-mail environment. But then the texts did not usually need to be more accurate than they were. In terms of the communicative event, messages were perfectly understood. As real-world users of e-mail, we are aware of this emergence of talky-writing. Whilst accepting that the same conventions associated with writing to different audiences will still apply, as we become more familiar with the recipient, inaccuracies are tolerated.

More importantly for our considerations here is the content of the messages. Here are two successive messages from one learner. The second had been preceded by an intervening reply from his partner.

Hello Jane my name is amar i am a student at kings high school this is my first time i am using e -mail i have a hight of 5.5 foot i am 13 years old i live with my mum, dad, gran , 3 brothers, 1 sister.
looking forward to your reply.

Hello Jane this is amar I recived your reply to my first letter . You want to know what my brothers & sister are like the oldest child ln my family is my brother and he is 16 on Nov the 28 he is called Nasir he will be taking G.C.S.E exams this year. I am the next oldest and I am 13. After me there is my younger brother who is 6 in Jan the 13 his name is Vakas. After him ther is my youngest brother who is 4 his name is Wakar. The youngest and most spoilt (becauceshe is the only girl) is 2 on Nov 27 her name is Arooj. Me and my oldest brother live with my gran the rest live with my mum.
Looking forwerd to hearing from you.

It is clear that the learner is being prompted for more information ('you want to know what my brothers and sisters are like'), and this he provides. All the learners, to varying degrees, developed their ideas in response to prompting and questions. In a more traditional context, we would respond to learners' written texts in a similar way, encouraging development of content. The difference here is that the text or rather *texts* developed over time. The texts were in fact chunks of ideas that the learners generated on a theme as they corresponded.

As the learners moved towards the publishing of their autobiographies on their web page, various key aspects were apparent:

– the learners moved back to the word processor as their writing tool
– the teachers involved in the e-mail communications began to act as *readers of texts*, not as correspondents
– the learners edited their texts and were closely supported by their teachers
– the learners included the information they had 'rehearsed' within their e-mail exchanges

The latter point is best illustrated in the following messages from one of the learners from Mongolia. From message one to message two, there is a clear development in sentence complexity, although the overall accuracy is still faulty. The second message responds to prompting from his partner for more information.

MESSAGE 1

Hello ?
How is your studying ?
My name is Maizorig and I came from Mongolia .The Mongolia is between Russia and China . Mongolia is very big country but just two and half million people live in this country .I'am fifteen years old . I have a brother . He goes to Unversity of Mongolia . My father is doctor . Now I live with my mother in students' flat . I came in Manchester just seven months ago . I am realy happy in writing to you mail .s.p : Sorry about my English .

MESSAGE 2

Today I am so happy because of your message.
I came from Mongolia which is located between Russia and China. My country has a 2 and half million people. Mongolia is ex-comunnist country and since 1990 everything has changed. Mongolia is three times begger than France and if you go there you will feel like in Scotland. I live in capital city and every summer I go to my grandmother's home who lives in countryside. I have black and short hair. Not tall and look like funny. I am fifteenyears old and this may I will be sixteeen.My hobbies are ride a horse, read about history like World war-2, play table tennis and go to trip.

Maizorig's contribution for the web page reflects the content of these two messages and he also had help from the language support teacher with his word processing. He sent the final text to his partner for reading and comment (the first part is reproduced over).

Hello again. I am so happy that sending information about me for you. I hope that you will have an interest in my shot story.

MY HISTORY

I was born in the Mongolian countryside. Mongolia is an ex-Communist country which is located between China and Russia. Mongolia is three times bigger than France. In fact I don't know about the first few years of my childhood. Sometimes my parents tell me some memories of my childhood. We moved to the capital city and since that time I can remember something about me.

My father and mother were doctors. I have one brother and he is 20 years old now. My grandmother lives in the countryside of Mongolia. Every summer I go to the countryside for help her. In the countryside everything is nice. It is a beautiful and natural place with fresh air. I like to ride a horse when I am in the countryside. I came to High School on 26th April. That day I met my new friends and new school at first.

What does this tell us about the writing tools available to us? Are e-mail and the World Wide Web in fact writing tools? How should we use them in relation to the word processor? Thinking about these tools in relation to the process of writing may go some way towards helping us to define appropriate roles for them within our writing curricula.

E-mail, for example, is a transporter of information and ideas. In real world usage, the message is all important; an L1 user will often transgress the rules of accuracy, perhaps unwittingly, but sometimes deliberately, missing out capitalisation or punctuation to save time. If a message is unclear or incomplete, clarification or extension is sought as it would be in spoken contexts. There is an opportunity to continue the 'dialogue', to generate and develop ideas.

The norms of writing to be read and immediately understood by a wider audience, however, also bring with them expectations of accuracy and text organisation. By allowing us to draft and edit text, the word processor facilitates the production of acceptable text.

And the World Wide Web? This simply provides an alternative publication arena, an arena that resembles the electronic version of the 'class newspaper on the wall' idea.

Here is another brief example, to illustrate this conceptual framework as applied to a writing exchange between two groups of learners.

The two learner groups were 11- to 12-year-olds in their first year of secondary education, each in a different school and each school being in a different education authority. There were also high numbers of second language learners in each of the groups; however, given the geographical locations of the schools, the ethnic communities represented were in fact quite different too.

The children were linked up with each other by e-mail and the purpose of the exchange was both to have an opportunity to communicate with peers beyond their own school environment and to exchange ideas and texts on a topic that was part of their English curriculum: the writing of folk or fairy tales. Given the ethnic cultures represented by the two groups, we felt that this could develop into a fruitful area of exchange. Based on the framework that I have described in the previous project, those stories would be developed using word processing and finally published on a shared web page for peer readership and perhaps beyond. This is a sequence of activities based on how this writing project evolved:

- Teachers initiate pre-writing work on the genre of folk tales; the children spend time reading and comprehending other stories.
- Link-ups between children in the two schools and initial exchange of 'getting-to-know-you messages'.
- Teachers support children in beginning to generate ideas and introductions to their stories.
- Children begin to share ideas over e-mail. (These may be ideas for the stories they are inventing or they may begin to recount stories from their own cultures, especially fruitful if the learners involved are from different areas around the world or even different ethnic communities within one country, as was the case in our project.)
- Learners continue to develop their stories using the word processor. (Drafts of early stages can be sent to the learners' e-mail partners. Depending on the learner groups, responses may be more or less sophisticated.)
- When happy with their stories, learners publish them on a web site, ideally for the peer e-mail partners to read from their own location.

Here is a flavour of the resulting web site of one of the groups I have mentioned.

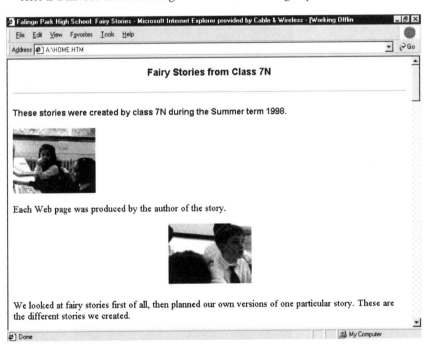

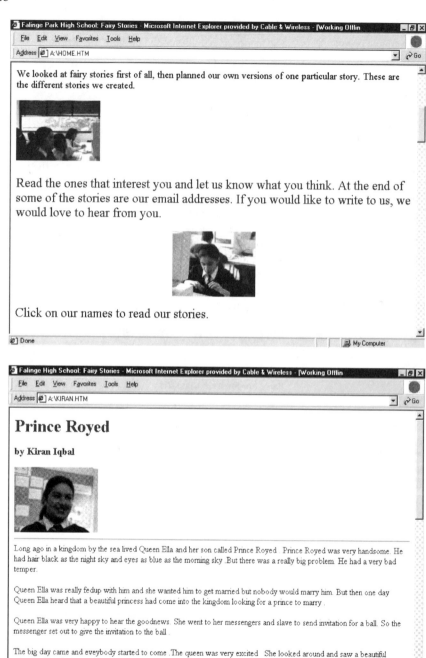

We looked at fairy stories first of all, then planned our own versions of one particular story. These are the different stories we created.

Read the ones that interest you and let us know what you think. At the end of some of the stories are our email addresses. If you would like to write to us, we would love to hear from you.

Click on our names to read our stories.

Prince Royed

by Kiran Iqbal

Long ago in a kingdom by the sea lived Queen Ella and her son called Prince Royed. Prince Royed was very handsome. He had hair black as the night sky and eyes as blue as the morning sky. But there was a really big problem. He had a very bad temper.

Queen Ella was really fedup with him and she wanted him to get married but nobody would marry him. But then one day Queen Ella heard that a beautiful princess had come into the kingdom looking for a prince to marry.

Queen Ella was very happy to hear the goodnews. She went to her messengers and slave to send invitation for a ball. So the messenger set out to give the invitation to the ball.

The big day came and eveybody started to come. The queen was very excited. She looked around and saw a beautiful princess. Then he just came down the stairs and stood beside the princess.

The children put together their individual pages and a keen editorial group linked the collection from a simple but clear menu. These were then posted up on the school website.

Writing for the Web will also ultimately involve different ways of writing; it will involve writing 'hypertextually' which brings further challenges and huge creative opportunities for learners. Bicknell (1999) describes how his learners produced pages about their institution and its host community for prospective students based on the prompt 'Before you came to the United States, what questions did you have about West Virginia University and Morgantown?' The multiple aspects of the pages provided an ideal project for collaborative practice and for multi-skills work of an authentic nature. This teacher used an HTML editor as did we with the children, but given the ease with which we can achieve hyperlinked documents through word processors such as Microsoft *Word* nowadays, the potential to publish in this way, as opposed to printing out on paper, is far easier than before.

Alternatively there are websites dedicated to writing exchange and to which learners can send their work for posting, obviously to be read by a wider and perhaps more unfamiliar audience. These may be of interest to you and your learners. Two examples are:
– The Pizzaz pages at http://darkwing.uoregon.edu/~leslieob/pizzaz.html
and
– The E-mail Project pages at http://www.otan.dni.us/webfarm/emailproject/email.htm

You may also find a site of relevance to your learners from the Yahoo links to Interactive fiction, on-line stories to which writers from around the world can contribute (http://dir.yahoo.com/Recreation/Games/Internet_Games/Web_Games/Interactive_Fiction/).

As can be seen, computers now have much to offer the writing teacher. Each tool has a role to play in encouraging learners to want to write and in helping learners to develop their writing skill. However, it is still worth emphasising that none of these technologies will fulfil their potential save for two key factors: the teacher and the task. Writing technologies will not sustain motivation in their own right. Teachers who design appropriate and authentic tasks in recognition of their learners' needs, abilities, and of the specific potentials of these technologies, will.

References

Bangert-Drowns R (1993) The word processor as an instructional tool: a meta-analysis of word processing in writing instruction *Review of Educational Research 63/1*

Beauvois M H (1997) High tech, high touch: from discussion to composition in the networked classroom *Computer Assisted Language Learning 10/1*

Bicknell J (1999) Promoting writing and computer literacy skills through student-authored web pages *TESOL Journal* Spring 1999

Chandler D (1993) Writing strategies and writers' tools *English Today 34, 9/3*

Cochran-Smith M (1991) Wordprocessing and writing in the elementary classroom: a critical review of related literature *Review of Educational Research 61/1*

Daiute C (1985) *Writing and Computers* Addison-Wesley

Davis P & M Rinvolucri (1988) *Dictation* Cambridge University Press

Hyland K (1993) ESL Computer writers: what can we do to help? *System 21/1*

Jacobs G (1986) Quickwriting: a technique for invention in writing *ELTJ 40/3*

Kroonenberg N (1995) Developing communicative and thinking skills via e-mail *TESOL Journal 4/2*

Lam F S & M Pennington (1995) The computer vs the pen: a comparative study of word processing in a Hong Kong secondary classroom *Computer Assisted Language Learning 8/1*

Neu J & R Scarcella (1991) Word processing in the ESL writing classroom. In Dunkel P (Ed.) (1991) *Computer Assisted Language Learning and Testing* Harper Collins

Pennington M (1996) Writing the natural way: *Computer Assisted Language Learning 9/2-3*

Phinney M (1989) Computers, composition and second language teaching. In Pennington M (Ed.) *Teaching Languages with Computers: The State of the Art* Athelstan

Piper A (1987) Helping learners to write: a role for the word processor *ELTJ 41/2*

Scrimshaw P (1993) Co-operative writing with computers. In Scrimshaw P (Ed.) (1993) *Language, Classrooms and Computers* Routledge

Slaouti D (1998) Motivating learners to write: a role for email *CALL Review* January 1998

Slaouti D (forthcoming 2000) In search of a role for email and the World Wide Web in improving writing. In O'Brien T & M Beaumont (Eds.) *Collaborative Research in Second Language Learning* Trentham Books

Soh B L & Y P Soon (1991) English by e-mail: creating a global classroom via the medium of computer technology *ELT Journal 45/4*

Sullivan N & E Pratt (1996) A comparative study of two ESL writing environments: a computer-assisted classroom and a traditional oral classroom *System 29/4*

Swan M & C Walter (1990) *Cambridge English Course 2* Cambridge University Press

Warschauer M (1996) *Motivational aspects of using computers for writing and communication* (on-line) Second Language Teaching and Curriculum Centre, University of Hawaii http://www.lll.hawaii.edu/nflrc/NetWorks/NW01.html

Warschauer M, L Turbee & B Roberts (1996) Computer learning networks and student empowerment *System 24/1*

2 Practical uses for language corpora in ELT

Dr Christopher Tribble

Dr Christopher Tribble is a freelance consultant based in London and Colombo, Sri Lanka, where he is involved in the design, management and evaluation of education reform projects. He has been an IATEFL member since 1985 and has written for both *Muesli News* and *CALL Journal* on uses of corpora in ELT. He is currently an Associate Lecturer of King's College, London University, and teaches courses in 'English for Academic Purposes', and 'Discourse, Genre, Style, Corpora' on the MA in Applied Linguistics and ELT at King's. Apart from conference papers and articles, he has published on the teaching of writing and corpus applications in language education with Longman, Oxford University Press, and Athelstan.   christopher_tribble@compuserve.com
ctribble@sri.lanka.net
http://ourworld.compuserve.com/homepages/Christopher_Tribble

Corpora in the classroom – state of play

It is possible, but by no means certain, that most teachers of English to speakers of other languages have heard about corpora by now. If they have, they will know that a corpus is a collection of texts which are held on computer and which can be analysed for purposes of language description. Those teachers who have come to recent IATEFL conferences will have listened to linguists and dictionary makers like John Sinclair, Michael Rundell and Della Summers talk about the multi-million word (and pound) projects in which they have been involved and they will have (maybe) been impressed by the things you can do with the British National Corpus or the Bank of English. The many who have never been to a teachers' conference will possibly have seen and used modern corpus-based dictionaries like those published by Collins COBUILD and Longman. Most teachers may even agree that they, and their students, have benefited from the improvements in learners' dictionaries and grammars which the 'corpus revolution' has made possible. However, despite the best efforts of people like Tim Johns, Guy Aston, John Flowerdew and myself (see the bibliography) not many teachers seem to be *using* corpora in their classrooms.

Why should this be? First, there is the reality that teachers work in an increasingly pressured environment – especially in the private sector. If you are teaching 20 or more classes a week, and if you need to stick to an agreed curriculum, you have very little time for materials development or methodological innovation. Secondly, it is my experience that there is still a high level of techno-fear out there. Very few teachers own a computer – they do not see it as an essential professional tool – and many are frightened off by the sales staff who try to sell them a Ferrari when all they need is a delivery van[1]. And those who do have access to computers are still surprisingly ignorant about how the PC can make life easier. I have recently run staff development sessions in a number of overseas universities, and I have been struck by the low level of basic knowledge many language teachers have even about their word processor. Hands up if you know how to create multi-level numbered paragraphs, have left and right justified text on the same line, or sort a wordlist. Hands up if you are a happy spreadsheet user. Hands up if you even care one way or the other! Is it a surprise that not many teachers are using corpora? However, this chapter aims to address these issues and to help teachers to be able to incorporate the use of corpora into their lessons.

What is the right corpus for ELT?

Getting the answer to this question right is the most important thing to do when starting to use corpora in language teaching. We will focus on two possible aspects of language teaching: vocabulary and grammar teaching in a general English programme, and an ESP course – say business communication or an ESP or EAP programme for post-graduate students.

General English

Grammar and vocabulary in general English

In this kind of programme your focus as a teacher might be to provide students with an accessible and rapid means of extending their understanding of how certain words work. For example, assume that students in a lower level group keep on putting *already* in inappropriate places in their writing (or speaking), like this:

The most unloved person who ever lived was Sue. When Sue was born her parents did not want her as they <u>had already</u> ten children to look after.

With the right kind of corpus you will be able to give them a printout like the one below in Table 1, and ask them to say in which part of the clause this word seems to be found. On the evidence to hand, learners should spot that in most instances *already* either comes between an auxiliary and a verb or in front of the verb, unless the verb is copula *be* – '22 […] it's already too late' – and be able to form a provisional rule for the use of the word.

This kind of activity has various advantages:
a) it takes very little time to prepare (assuming you have the right kind of corpus to hand)
b) it provides contextualised instances of use which are readily accessible to learners,
c) it lets them develop rules that are memorable because they are based on experience, and
d) it can be kept as a reference resource for later use.

The corpus used for generating these examples is the *British National Corpus Sampler* (OUCS, 1999). This is a collection of approximately one million words of written English

1.	pe Section 60 Public Health Act 1936	already	applies to warehouses which have &b
2.	e week after I 'll have a wife, one	already	arranged for and waiting. What do yo
3.	ia the electronic technology that is	already	available, or alternatively people coul
4.	s the chance that your friends might	already	be a bunch of werewolves, vampires,
5.	US garrison of about 10,000 men had	already	been augmented to 13,000 before airb
6.	l to the Coquelles terminal site has	already	been driven and work on the southern
7.	variable, be uniformly ordered have	already	been explained. Most of the other co
8.	the enclave. The diplomatic one has	already	begun. But Lebanon 's inter-commun
9.	last financial year. With staffing	already	cut to the bone, it was union membe
10.	ould prove highly detrimental to the	already	disgraced former East German leader
11.	ven above. By virtue of what we have	already	established, the following proposition
12.	en, and Elisabeth saw that they were	already	grouped together on the shore. Baltic
13.	he original shareholders. They have	already	lost their cash. The company is now
14.	rm Mrs Thatcher. President Bush has	already	promised that no commitments will b
15.	a similar effect. American insurers	already	reckon there is a $40bn – about
16.	public. Around 1,000 customers have	already	rung the share information line on 080
17.	nd CAR). Thus the procedure we have	already	set up will work when given a program
18.	ser are dealing with a narrative not	already	shaped into theatrical scenes. Berg '
19.	of the UK 's industrial giants have	already	slashed costs and wages to the bone
20.	e severe for other regions which are	already	suffering the effects of the socalled N
21.	married the deceased when he was	already	suffering from a fatal disease and she
22.	safety. I think it's	already	too late for that. Karen spent
23.	e for his surplus will include votes	already	transferred at earlier stages. To exa
24.	e else subscribed to. Your cell was	already	waiting for you. How could you endur
25.	on existing, traditional industries	already	within the government 's fiscal philoso

Table 1 A concordance of already *taken from the British National Corpus Sampler – written sub-set*

and one million words of spoken English taken from the *British National Corpus* (OUCS, 1995). The *Sampler* follows the same structure as the *BNC* – i.e. an attempt has been made to include a representative sample of a range of written and spoken genres and other contextually determined text categories.

For searches involving common items, the *BNC Sampler* is ideal. It can be used directly from the CD-ROM, it is inexpensive (£50), it comes complete with various tools (more of these anon), and, importantly, it doesn't give you too much data. For most grammatically oriented learning/teaching, the *BNC Sampler* is fine[2]. Good examples of the kinds of research students can do are:

– *for, since* and *ago*
– how writers (or speakers) use logical connectors
– finding out about multi-word verbs (e.g. *get up to*)

BNC Sampler data for the last of these is given on the next page. It offers a good instance of the amount of information you can get from search results which have been sorted to the right. The first task to ask students to carry out would be to identify which of these instances are and are not three-word verbs. The second task would be to ask them to confirm meaning(s) associated with the three-word verb itself in these contexts.

10004	ve a few jars over Christmas and they	get up to	all sorts of things in the house do
10005	at . And what sort of things did you	get up to?	Er well we had er er a very fine
10006	heck that the Did I tell me when we	got up to	erm Newcastle we turned on the loca
10007	n during the interval, the crocodile	got up to	go to the toilet. I must say
10008	His face is black, whatever do you	get up to	in the car?' 'Mum, Charlotte, mum rig
10009	emembered the observatory. You could	get up to	it by the stairs to the roof. He 'd
10010	and That 's all? Yeah and when she	got up to	leave he just like patted her on th
10011	n chairs and an important-looking man	got up to	speak. He said nice things about t
10012	e top of the house Ah. but when we	got up to	the top of the house I needed to go
10013	ashioned values? As children, we all	got up to	tricks like pinching a few apples o

Table 2 A concordance of got up to from the BNC Sampler

While the *BNC Sampler* can be very helpful with this kind of vocabulary enrichment, if a student wants to find out how rarer or slang words are used (e.g. *bottle* (n.) = courage/determination '*got a lot of bottle*') a corpus might not be the right answer to their problem. To begin with, they may not find what they are looking for – a corpus is only a sample of language in use – it can never be *the* language[3]. And while the full *BNC* may contain examples of the form that you seek, the huge amount of non-examples which will also come up is going to take so much time to go through that neither you nor your students are going to think the effort is worthwhile. In this case, forget about the corpus and reach for the dictionary – you might as well benefit from the research that others have done.

So far we have seen that for General English teaching a corpus like the *BNC Sampler* can be an appropriate source of language information, but that for more specific vocabulary it may not be so useful. From the perspective of the general English student is this the end of the story? Fortunately not – enter the CD-ROM Encyclopaedia!

More specialised vocabulary

Many teachers and students will have used a CD-ROM Encyclopaedia as a reference work. While they may have taken advantage of the search facilities these publications provide and used specific texts as reading materials, it seems that few if any are using the texts as a source of linguistic data. I have argued elsewhere (Tribble C, 1997) that there can be specific advantages in using CD-ROM reference works in such a way. The mechanics of searching, copying and pasting text from a CD-ROM into Windows Notepad are very straightforward. Once encyclopaedia entries are in this editable form, texts can be saved as files in an appropriate sub-directory and constitute the basis for a specialist micro-corpus.

As an example, consider the case of a group of students who are confused by the difference between *practice* and *practise* in British English. A mixed micro-corpus containing a mix of business, sports and health related texts can provide rapid exemplification of the contrast between these two words (a contrast which often confuses mother-tongue users of English as well). Students can be presented with concordance output such as that given below (Table 3) and asked to elaborate a 'rule' for the use of the two words.

1.	s of enabling students to understand and	practise	specific physical skills so that a high
2.	nced or registered, he or she is free to	practise	the profession in any country which reco
3.	be descendants of the god of medicine,	practised	a form of psychotherapy called incubati
4.	e (1602), Harvey returned to England and	practised	medicine in the London area. He was ele
5.	denounced some of Galen's teachings and	practised	simplified treatment of dislocations, f
6.	exotic fish for pure pleasure has been	practised	since ancient times; today it ranks as
7.	hythm and coordination through routines	practised	with hoops, clubs, and small balls. G
8.	In 1858, Dickens had begun the lucrative	practice	of reading publicly from his own work, a
9.	, constituted the core of the theory and	practice	of Bolshevism and the Third Internationa
10.	asingly important international business	practice.	In 1988, for example, 13 US advertising
11.	well organized, the sharp and unethical	practices	of some advertisers prompted the passin
12.	ss endeavour. The use of sales promotion	practices	has experienced steady growth in the 20
13.	motional tactics. Warranty and guarantee	practices,	in particular, have been closely exami
14.	not identical with accounting theory and	practices.	Tax regulations are based on laws that
15.	ities to hired personnel became a common	practice,	financial reporting began to focus on s
16.	st a different result. An example is the	practice	of consolidating the financial statement
17.	entually, the public outcry against such	practices	was great enough in the United States t
18.	ons are based on fee-for-service private	practice.	Physicians and other practitioners cont
19.	and physical) afforded by the study and	practice	of martial arts (for example, judo, kara

Table 3 A concordance of practice/practise

The advantages of a CD-ROM encyclopaedia micro-corpus in this instance are that a) the texts are presented in contexts that are interesting and accessible for the learners, and b) although the corpus is small it offers *sufficient* (rather than overwhelming) data.

English for specific learning purposes

The example of ways in which a corpus of texts from a CD-ROM encyclopaedia can be used to develop learning materials for learners with an interest in more specific areas of language-in-use provides a good entry point for this next section. Students with specific learning purposes present a particular challenge to teachers – and appropriate text corpus resources can be particularly helpful in such teaching/learning settings.

For this group however, neither *BNC Sampler* nor the full *BNC* really represent a satisfactory resource – they have been compiled with a view to allowing generalisations to be made about current British English, not to providing examples for language teaching. Students and teachers on specific purposes programmes require different kinds of text resources. These can be called *exemplar* and *analogue* corpora (Tribble C, forthcoming).

An exemplar corpus will contain texts which have closely similar communicative purposes and which are generically congruent with the texts the students want to learn how to write. Examples of these kinds of text genres might be:

- Brochures for products or courses
- Grant applications submitted to the Engineering and Science Research Council
- MA dissertations in social sciences
- Offer letters for life insurance

An analogue corpus will contain texts which, while they are not identical in communicative purpose and generic convention, are as close as you can get for your immediate pedagogic purpose. Such a corpus might be useful for a teacher who faces the problem of developing a corpus of relevant text exemplars for students who come from a wide range of disciplinary backgrounds (as in many ESP/EAP programmes). The logistics of obtaining a fully representative exemplar corpus of the text genres a mixed group of students may need to know about can be impossibly difficult. In such circumstances it becomes necessary to collect examples of texts that are sufficiently 'like' the desired target genres to meet the broad needs of the group.

Business communication

For students on a business communications programme, the analysis of an exemplar corpus can offer insights not only into the ways in which specific lexical items are used, but also help us to understand the positions which are ascribed to participants in a discourse. For example, in a recent study of 'Web Brochures' for MA programmes in ELT/Applied Linguistics (Tribble C, forthcoming), it was possible to discover that *student(s)* and *course* have outstandingly high frequency when compared with other texts, but take on contrasting roles in the discourse. An analysis of the collocates of *student/ students* tells us that in this particular environment students *take, produce, choose, follow, work, write,* and that they do these things in the present – or timeless future. A study of *course* (Table 4) shows us a very different picture. For a start the word frequently appears in theme position in the clauses in which it is found. Secondly, 8 out of 23 instances are agentless passives, two are passives with agent, one is copula *be* and in thirteen instances *course* is given animate attributes by being allowed to *examine, include, introduce, look at, prepare, provide,* or *set out to explore.*

```
The course includes presentations by [a]
This course also introduces students t [a]
This course introduces students to a [a]
This course introduces students to cur [a]
This course introduces students to res [a]
The course introduces the major theor [a]
The course is the result of [a]
This course looks at issues and tech [a]
This course prepares students for their [a]
This course prepares students for their [a]
The course also provides a sound ba [a]
The course sets out to explore the th [a]
The course will also examine relation [a]
The course programme for each ten-week programme is based on [p]
The course is designed for teachers [p]
The course is intended for language t [p]
This course is designed for working t [p]
The course is organised [p]
This course is organised in three part [p]
The course will be organised thematic [p]
Other courses may also be on offer – [p]
This course is mainly taught by mem [p + agent]
The course is taught by means of lec [p + agent]
```

Table 4 A concordance of course *using data from web brochures*

An apprentice writer tasked with the writing of a promotional brochure of this kind would gain at least two important insights from this kind of study. First, they would come to an understanding of the roles which writers have decided to ascribe to two of the major 'participants' in the MA process – students, and the course. Secondly they would have access to the lexis and phrase structure which these writers and their departments have considered appropriate to the genre they were planning to write into. Such an analysis does not place an obligation on learners to write in the same way as the writers of the texts in the corpus. However, a decision to write in a *different* way can now be informed by an understanding of the state-of-the-art, and will represent the writer's conscious decision to strike out on their own.

EAP

While students in EAP writing programmes can gain similar insights from the use of exemplar corpora – e.g. the study of citations in academic writing (Thompson, P & C Tribble, 1999), it can often be extremely difficult to build exemplar corpora for use by this group. Where do you find publicly available instances of examination scripts? In these circumstances it can be more practical to work with an *analogue corpus*. One of the best examples of a learning programme based on this kind of corpus can be found in Tim Johns' 'Data Driven Learning Library' at http://sun1.bham.ac.uk/johnstf/ddl_lib.htm. The materials on this site have been developed for a course at Birmingham University which Johns describes as follows:

> Remedial Grammar is an elective lunch-time class that meets twice a week during the Autumn Term, and once during the Spring Term. It is linked to the syntactic areas defined in the Birmingham Assessment and Diagnostic Test taken by all international students on arrival at the University. (Johns: ibid.)

What Johns does not say is that the programme is hugely successful with students and – despite its rather austere title – attracts large numbers of students each term. An example of a small part of the materials used in the course is given in Table 5 on the next page.

The corpus which has been used in the development of these materials comprises comparatively distant analogues of the kinds of writing that students need to do – many of the texts coming from the *New Scientist*. While I have argued against the use of this kind of journalistic text as an explicit *model* for teaching writing (Tribble C, forthcoming), because of its accessibility and interest value it has many advantages as a basis for the development of motivatingly contextualised remedial activities such as the example given above. Clearly, CD-ROM encyclopaedia-based activities could also be used to similar effect.

Zero Article

In this handout we look at 5 'key nouns' in English which may be countable **or** uncountable (**industry, language, society, trade** and **religion**), together with a sixth (**literature**) which is similar in the way it behaves, though there the difference in countability is not so clear. For each noun, 1–3 pairs of citations are given to help you try to work out the difference in **meaning** between the noun as countable and as uncountable, and 12 'gapped' citations to see if you have formed the correct hypothesis (key provided at the end).

---

industry

1. Last year output of **the electronics industry** rose 28 per cent on an employment rise of only 3 per cent.
2. **The British film industry** has always had a problem trying to film in the great British outdoors.
3. It opened in 1985 as the bequest of the prime minister, Andrei Kozygin, to the town and to **Soviet light industry**.
4. Further rises will mean deep trouble for Toyota, as for most of **Japanese industry**.

```
 1.      they would all get jobs in _____ British industry, Still more alarmist about the flow
 2.      ne lead-free fuel. And _____ British car industry, in the face of mounting environment
 3.      ith the huge expansion in _____ chemical industry that took place after the Second Wor
 4.    and on Hunt's knowledge of _____ modern industry, It is lavishly ilustrated, partly i
 5.      research on new ideas in _____ European industry. One of the major aims of the shake-
 6.        for storage heaters). _____ electricity industry does not intend to make a habit of c
 7.    o seek firm proposals from _____ private industry to take over the government's remote
 8.       olic work. Glucose is used by _____ food industry mainly in the manufacture of confect
 9.      rea used to be the centre of _____ heavy industry. For 100 years after 1830, when the
10.     ical profession and _____ pharmaceutical industry has tottered from crisis to crisis n
11. management, such as _____ manufacturing industry, local authorities, reclamation and
12.      left _____ French information-technology industry in a mess – at least compared with A
```

Table 5 A Handout from Remedial Grammar Course *by Tim Johns*

Corpus resources – summary

So far, we have seen that three kinds of corpus resources might be useful for language teachers and students. The general corpus can be used as a basis for programmes designed to help students extend language, grammar and lexical awareness. In contrast to the general corpus, exemplar and analogue corpora can be of particular value in the development of programmes for learners with more specific needs.

What hardware and software do we need?

Hardware

Whatever corpus resources you have been able to assemble, you (or your students) will still have to undertake research and then make the results of that research available. Fortunately, the hardware requirements for this sort of work are no more than the 'entry level' for a new PC – or well below[4]. Assuming you are working with a modern

Windows PC with a CD-ROM drive (there is software available for Macintosh PCs but it is very restricted), and that a basic printer is connected to the computer, you have all the hardware you need to start working with corpora.

Software

Two kinds of software are required to do corpus research. The first is a concordancing package (output from which has already been shown above). For a Windows PC there are only two real options – WordSmith Tools (Scott M, 1996, 1998 – more information at http://www.liv.ac.uk/~ms2928/homepage.html and MonoConc 1.5 or MoncConc Pro for Windows (Barlow M, 1996, 1998 – more information at http://www.athel.com/). Using the basic functions of these programmes you will be able to make wordlists and concordances – the fundamentals of corpus study. MonoConc 1.5 has been designed with student use in mind, the 'Pro' version being more useful for research applications – though still very easy to use. WordSmith Tools is a more comprehensive program (a 'Swiss army knife for text analysis' according to the author Mike Scott) and has more functions than most learners (or teachers) will use, although these never get in the way of using the core programs in the suite. The feature which perhaps makes it stand out from anything else in the market is its 'Keyword' program (Scott M, 1997). This makes it possible for users to identify the statistically 'prominent' words or phrases in a text – as we have seen in *student* and *course* above this can be an invaluable resource in genre analysis.

The good news about the second kind of software that you need is that you probably already have it – a standard *Office* suite with a word processor and a spreadsheet. This provides the tools you need to deal with the results that you get back from your searches. The word processor makes it possible for you to re-format and edit the results you get from your concordancing software. The spreadsheet is invaluable when it comes to dealing with the quantification and analysis of results.

Conclusion

I commented on the many attempts to popularise a corpus-informed approach to language learning and teaching in the introduction to this chapter and will not revisit this argument here. Print accounts of what you can do and how you can do it are easily available and all very accessible (Aston G, 1997 and Boswood T, 1997 offer useful summaries of the state of play). The Web contains other sources of inspiration – worth mentioning are Cathy Ball's Georgetown University 'Tutorial: Concordances and Corpora' http://www.georgetown.edu/cball/corpora/tutorial.html, and the excellent Tim John's Data Driven Learning pages at http://sun1.bham.ac.uk/johnstf/ddl_lib.htm.

I hope that the comments I have made on the kinds of corpora you might want to use, and the overview of some of the benefits that can arise from this study, will encourage you to start using corpora in your own work. Once you have started, you will wonder how you ever managed to put together teaching materials without them.

Notes

[1] In the UK it is possible (June 1999) to buy an entry level PC for under £700 – and you'll probably get a printer, modem (for internet/e-mail connection) thrown in for the price. Such a machine will be more than adequate for a teacher whose main concerns are their own domestic administration and strengthening their teaching.

[2] See Biber D, S Conrad & R Reppen (1994) for an argument in favour of small corpora in the investigation of grammatical features of English.

[3] Thus, there are no examples of this sense of the word in the 114 instances in *BNC Sampler.*

[4] It is, in fact, possible to carry out very useful corpus research on early model PCs running under MS-DOS or Windows 3.1x.

Bibliography

Aston G (1996) Corpora in language pedagogy: matching theory and practice. In Cook G & B Seidlhofer (Eds.) *Principle and Practice in applied linguistics: Studies in honour of H G Widdowson* Oxford University Press

Aston G (1997) Enriching the learning environment: corpora in ELT. In Wichmann A, S Fligelstone, T McEnery & G Knowles (Eds.) *Teaching and language corpora* Longman

Biber D, S Conrad & R Reppen (1994) Corpus-based approaches to issues in Applied Linguistics *Applied Linguistics 15 2*

Boswood T (Ed.) (1997) *New Ways in using Computers in ESL* TESOL

Flowerdew J (1996) Concordancing in Language Learning in Martha Pennington (Ed.) *The Power of CALL* Athelstan

Granger S & C Tribble (1997) Exploiting Learner Corpus Data in the Classroom: form-focused instruction and data-driven learning in Granger S (Ed.) *Learner Language on Computer* Longman

Johns T (1991) Should you be persuaded: Two examples of Data-Driven Learning Materials *English Language Research Journal (University of Birmingham) 4*

Johns T (1994) From printout to handout: grammar and vocabulary learning in the context of data-driven learning in Odlin T (Ed.) *Approaches to Pedagogic Grammar* Cambridge University Press

Johns T (1997) Kibbitzing one-to-ones in Langley G V (Ed.) *BALEAP professional interest meetings report 1995–1997* British Association of Lecturers in English for Academic Purposes

Oxford University Computer Service (1995) *The British National Corpus* OUCS

Oxford University Computer Service (1999) *The British National Corpus Sampler* OUCS

Scott M (1997) PC Analysis of key words – and key key words *System 25 1*

Sinclair J (1987) *Looking Up* Collins ELT

Sinclair J (1991) *Corpus, Concordance, Collocation* Oxford University Press

Tribble C (1997) Corpora, Concordances and ELT in Boswood T (Ed.) *New Ways in using Computers in ESL* TESOL

Thompson P & C Tribble (1999) Exploring citation practices through corpus research paper presented at the CALS Silver Anniversary Seminar, Reading University

Tribble C & G Jones (1997) *Concordances in the Classroom: a resource book for teachers* Athelstan

Tribble C (1991) Some uses of electronic text in English for academic purposes in Millom, J C and K Tong (EOds.) *Text Analysis in Computer Assisted Language Learning* Hong Kong University of Science and Technology & City Polytechnic of Hong Kong

Tribble C (1997) Improvising corpora for ELT: quick-and-dirty ways of developing corpora for language teaching in Melia J & B Lewandowska-Tomaszczyk (Ed.) *PALC '97 Proceedings* Łódź University Press

Tribble C (forthcoming) Corpora and corpus analysis: new windows on academic writing. In Flowerdew J (Ed.) *Academic Discourse* Addison Wesley Longman

3 Using computer-based digital video in language learning

Dr Paul Brett

Dr Paul Brett served as Chair of the IATEFL Computer SIG from 1996 to 2000. He is a Senior Lecturer at the University of Wolverhampton and has published extensively on the applications of multimedia to language learning. He is also the author of two series of CD-ROMS *English for Business* (Phillips, 1997) and *Citizen of the World* (Phillips, 1998). He has undertaken many consultancies in computer-assisted language learning around the world.   P.Brett@wlv.ac.uk

Multimedia PCs are relatively new, but have become commonplace since the mid-1990s. With the introduction of digital TV and the expected increase in the speed and capacity of the World Wide Web, access to multimedia is inevitably going to expand. Digital video is a key language learning resource in the same way that analogue video is, and some of the techniques in this chapter apply equally to both types. However, the advantage of digital video which is delivered by the PC is that it can be surrounded by, and linked in with, other language learning materials. This chapter shows how computer-based digital video can be used in language learning, in particular for listening comprehension.

The chapter describes, briefly, how the ability of the computer to deliver video, and to amalgamate this with other media: sound, pictures, graphics and text, to create a multimedia environment, has advantages for a variety of areas of language learning. These are discussed in the light of several themes from Second Language Acquisition (SLA) theory, and then from research findings into the use of video, subtitled-video and multimedia. Teachers, with very little computer know-how, can now create their own multimedia lessons using transparent authoring packages, web page authoring, and even with word processors (see Lesson idea 1). The chapter considers some of the key pedagogic factors in the creation of video-based multimedia. There is then an overview of the sources, the advantages and disadvantages, and language learning task types which may be applied to digital video. The chapter concludes with four generic lesson ideas, all of which are based around digital video, and all of which can be adapted for any group of learners.

Why bother with multimedia?

SLA Theory and multimedia

The potential of multimedia fits well with ideas from SLA theory about how second language learning occurs, see Doughty (1991a), Chapelle (1997) and Chapelle (1998). The negotiated interaction model of SLA sees that it is the interactional modifications made upon raw language input to make it comprehensible which serve to facilitate acquisition. Multimedia-based materials can provide the resources which will enable learners to retrieve meaning from problematic input. These resources might provide the same types of information as would be available from a fluent speaker, i.e. clarification of the meanings of words or grammar. By augmenting input with a variety of learning support resources, e.g. on-line dictionaries, subtitles, and comprehension tasks with corrective feedback, learners may have the necessary resources with which to make any non-comprehensible input comprehensible (Chapelle, 1997: 27). Furthermore, the multimedia environment may provide clear access to the linguistic items which have caused comprehension breakdown, and the necessary resources to facilitate a negotiated understanding of the problematic linguistic items (Doughty, 1991a: 3).

A learner's conscious 'noticing' of the new features in linguistic input has been shown to predate and assist such items in being understood and eventually used (Schmidt and Frota, 1986). Doughty (1991b) showed how a computer environment designed to highlight relative clauses resulted in learning. The multimedia environment affords a variety of ways to make input, both written and aural, salient and noticeable. These include the use of cognitive tasks, the use of colour, the use of hyperlinked information or through transcriptions of spoken text.

Autonomous language learning, e.g. Dickinson (1987), is another theme which fits well with multimedia. A multimedia language learning application may be adapted by learners to accommodate their own language learning preferences. So, in addition to the choice of when to study, multimedia also provides learners with autonomy within each individual learning session. Learners can choose to focus on language areas that they decide they need help with and ignore others. They can take as much time as they like, and exploit whichever of the variety of media that they prefer to learn from. They can work at whatever pace they choose, and use or not use any off-line materials.

Research into the use of video, subtitled-video and multimedia on aspects of language learning

Research into the effects of the different media which may make up a multimedia environment has shown them to be positive. The use of video for listening comprehension generally shows enhanced comprehension. Among studies which confirm this are: Ramsey (1991), Secules et al. (1992), Baltova (1994) and Herron et al. (1995). However the effect of video on comprehension may depend on how the visual image supports the aural text, how consistent the visual imagery is with the aural text (Grimes, 1990) and how proficient the learners are. Research, then, indicates a positive role for multimedia. Studies into the use of subtitled-video show that these greatly enhance comprehension. Readers might like to see Guillory (1998), Garza (1991), or Danan (1992). All report on the positive effects of subtitled-video. Generally, studies of multimedia environments also show enhanced language learning. Borrás and Lafayette (1994) demonstrated improved spoken performance, while Chun and Plass (1996) found positive effects for the learning of vocabulary. Johnstone and Milne (1995) showed that multimedia increased use of communicative discourse in the classroom by both teachers and pupils. Multimedia has also been found to help listening comprehension and studies of note are Grezel and Sciarone (1994), Brett (1996), Brett (1997) and Liou (1997).

Space prevents a detailed report on these findings but it appears that the use of digital video incorporated into a multimedia environment might be used for the following reasons and purposes:

– for the delivery of input for listening comprehension
– to provide video which can be accompanied by listening comprehension tasks
– to allow interactive listening comprehension
– to enable listening comprehension to be individualised
– to motivate learners
– to free up the teacher for individual work with learners
– to provide an environment in which learners can negotiate their own understanding
– to provide self-access materials
– to replicate real-world experience by using authentic materials
– to allow access to paralinguistic gestures, the speakers' sex, age, appearance, relationships, dress, mood, cultural behaviour and setting for the interaction.

Things to consider when using digital video for creating language learning materials

Which video clips?

There are powerful linguistic and pedagogic arguments for authentic video clips. Porter and Roberts (1981) analysed listening texts from EFL textbooks and found them to differ from real-life speech in thirteen ways, such as too much information, clear enunciation, distinct turn-taking and structural repetition. Sinclair's (1991) corpus-based work in examining natural language from the Cobuild database showed the importance of collocation and idioms. Underwood (1989: 100) concludes that it is authentic listening material which provides '... a true representation of real, spontaneous speech ... which will make them (listeners) more able to cope with "real life" speech when they meet it outside the learning situation'. She advocates its use from early stages. The selection of types of video clips, of course, should be matched to the learners' purposes and needs, reflecting the situations in which learners need to perform outside the classroom. The great advances made in 'streamed video' in the last couple of years (see Lesson idea 4) make the use of up-to-the-minute video very easy. The dominant format here is *RealPlayer*™ software and further information about this can be obtained from http://www.real.com.

What tasks?

Tasks which accompany video aim to support, guide, focus and assist listeners to extract the meanings from the texts. Tasks need to be designed '... as aids to aural comprehension practice, directing the students' attention to "focal points" on the tape so that they will learn to listen more effectively' (Underwood, 1989: 4). Such comprehension support tasks are very different from the types of tasks which aim to test comprehension, see Sheerin (1987). Materials writers have been extremely inventive in devising interesting tasks to accompany listening texts, see Stokes (1984). In addition to tasks such as questions, there are a whole range of more pro-active tasks, for example, using maps, pictures, true/false, diagrams, and labelling. These can all be replicated in an interactive way on the computer. Outcomes to tasks are a key aspect of design because they are a

'... recognisable evaluation point in a learning activity' (Rost, 1990: 168). A task outcome will allow learners (and teachers) to be able to evaluate their interpretations of listening texts and match their interpretations against those of a fluent speaker, contributing to a qualitative development in the listening skill. Unsuccessful outcomes may be important in listening development, because realising the causes of misinterpretation focuses attention on specific problematic linguistic forms or may highlight inappropriate use of listening strategies.

Classroom approaches to listening comprehension typically involve a sequence of tasks, epitomised by Underwood's (1989) sequence of pre-listening, while-listening and post-listening tasks. A pre-listening or watching stage involves tasks which aim to prepare the listener by activating scripts, schemata, and both linguistic and background knowledge. Research by Teichart (1996) and Herron et al. (1998), which called such a stage the 'advance organiser', has demonstrated its value in increasing comprehension. This stage eases the processing load while watching. Underwood (1989: 112) lists eleven task types that can be used to prepare listeners for the texts they are about to hear. Follow-up post-watching tasks may focus around a linguistic or informational element in the text, and be integrated into the development of grammar, vocabulary or of other skills.

The final issue in the creation of tasks is their difficulty. This can be manipulated by altering listeners' purposes, responses and the support material (Anderson & Lynch, 1988). While-watching tasks need to reflect the nature of the text, and both need to reflect the interests of listeners. The tasks need to be achievable. The task external response is that action which is required of the listener but the accompanying internal response needs to replicate that of a real-life listener, i.e. understanding of the essential meanings in the text. Nunan (1989) sees a continuum of difficulty of learner response to tasks, going from a task which needs no response, through to ones needing listening with understanding in order to solve a problem using the information. The final element in shaping listening task difficulty is the type and amount of any support material provided to accompany the task. This may be illustrations, diagrams, photographs, grids, maps etc. All can be used in a computer environment.

Feedback to the tasks

Task feedback is an essential element in creating materials, and ways of doing this are included in the four lesson ideas below. Feedback on task success needs to be immediate, if not '... much of the value of discussing why students have missed things or made errors is lost' (Underwood, 1989: 73). The importance of feedback is that it helps learners 'notice the gap' between their L2 knowledge and control over such knowledge during interactive discourse.

Sources of video and audio texts for use in computer-based language learning tasks

This section begins the practical discussion of the use of digital video. It provides a brief overview of the sources of digital video which may be used for language learning.

EFL-specific CD-ROMs

The major source of video for off-the-shelf computer-based language learning work is the CD-ROM. There are many EFL-specific titles which include video and audio listening texts. Many are linked to best-selling coursebooks, e.g. *Europlus+ Reward* (1998) or *Interchange* (1998), and are not, therefore, wholly dedicated to the development of listening comprehension. Indeed they may not afford any listening texts which are not also available on the cassettes which accompany the coursebooks. There are a few titles, however, which are primarily dedicated to listening and the *English for Business* (1997) suite of six titles is one which exploits authentic and non-scripted footage. *Business Territory* (1997) is another which uses authentic video sequences. There is an authoritative review of the CD-ROMs currently on the market in *The CD-ROM Teachers' Handbook* (Sharma, 1998).

Non-EFL CD-ROMs

Video clips can also be found in a variety of other types of CD-ROMs. The most common are edutainment titles such as *Encarta 99, Cinemania, Hutchinson Encyclopaedia* etc. The advantage of these titles is that any video clips are likely to be accompanied by thematically related pictures, texts, diagrams, music etc. They are usually of a very high quality, as might be expected of companies such as Microsoft.

CD-ROMs which are distributed free on the covers of all personal computer magazines often have video clips in them. The example in Lesson idea 2 below uses a trailer from a well-known film taken from such a CD-ROM. Digital Video Discs (DVD), which are replacing CD-ROMs, can hold around ten times the amount of information of a CD-ROM. These will increase the quantity and variety of digital video which might be exploited for language learning.

Video files on CD-ROMs can be identified by their extension labels, the most common are .avi, .mov and increasingly .mpg. These can be viewed independently of the material which surrounds them, most commonly through *Media Player.* Mpg video files are of a higher quality than .avi, and lend themselves to full screen video.

Video and audio clips from the Internet

Video clips in .avi, .mov and .mpg formats can also be downloaded from the Internet. As these files are usually large, expect them to take some time to download. Be prepared to learn how use *Winzip* (downloadable from http://www.tucows.com) as these files are often found zipped up to make them smaller to be downloaded more quickly.

Real-time video from the Internet

A different source of video is that which can be played in real time from the Internet. The sophistication of this technology is increasing rapidly, as are the number of formats and the software needed to play these video clips. The players for such video clips also come as plug-ins or additional components of Internet browsers such as *Internet Explorer* or Netscape *Communicator*. The one used in Lesson idea 3 is *RealPlayer G7*™ which can be downloaded free from http://www.real.com. The video files in this format come with extension names such as .ram or .ra. Some versions of these players allow you to save the video clips on your hard disc after they have been played, some do not. The quality of such video clips depends on many factors, but mainly on the speed of one's connection to the Web. In general these are as good quality as .avi, .mov or .jpg formats.

Creating your own digital video

The other way to create digital video for use in computer-based listening work is to record your own, which is probably only for the real techies amongst us. There are a variety of approaches to this, at the high end there are procedures needing highly specialised equipment, and at the low end a desktop video camera (web cam) costing around £70 is sufficient to capture low-quality video.

Advantages and disadvantages of these sources of video

Advantages

One advantage of CD-ROM video is that it is usually of a high quality, having been professionally filmed. The clips which have been recorded for inclusion in EFL multimedia titles will usually have specific language learning uses in mind. The video clip in Lesson idea 2 below used a clip from a dedicated EFL CD-ROM, originally created to practise past tenses. As noted though, video in EFL-specific CD-ROMs is rarely authentic.

Video clips taken from edutainment multimedia CD-ROMs are usually accompanied with other information in an array of different media, text, sound, pictures, animations, or graphs. Thus a video clip from *Encarta* of President Kennedy's inaugural speech is accompanied by, and linked to, reading texts about his time in power, photos, and sound clips. These might be exploited as in the do-it-yourself worksheets in Lesson idea 3 below, although be careful to check the copyright situation.

Digital video clips also have the distinct advantage over video cassettes that one can cue up and rewind almost instantaneously. There are no long searches in fast forward or rewind mode. Digital video is also easier to edit than videotape which will need two machines, for example, to cut out a section. The clip in Lesson idea 2 was edited so as to avoid a risqué ten-second section.

If students are able to work on listening tasks individually on their own PC then this puts them in control over the input, allowing stopping, starting, and note-taking, unlike the one TV to whole class scenario. It thus allows for individualisation.

Disadvantages

EFL-specific CD-ROMs rarely contain authentic video footage and one finds contrived dialogues especially written to highlight specific language structures or vocabulary, see Porter and Roberts (1981) and Sinclair (1990: 5). In addition, you are likely to be tied into the tasks which are presented by the authors, these may not be suitable for your learners, or you may believe they are not useful and wish to create alternative tasks just as one might with any course-book materials. Lesson idea 3 below is a suggestion about how to do this.

It is not easy to network CD-ROMs, although there are ways and means of doing this. Therefore using one CD-ROM with a large class will prove difficult without using the network version, which is sometimes available, but not always. The smoothest solution is to have multiple copies of the CD-ROMs, but this is likely to be expensive at approximately £35 a copy, depending on the titles. The price trend for CD-ROMs though is ever downwards!

If one selects one's own video clips and ways to exploit them, as in Lesson idea 2 below, then the video clip has to be copied on to the hard disc of the computer. Video clips are large and can eat up hard disc space voraciously.

The quality of digital video is usually not that of TV and video tape, although again this is improving rapidly with the advances in processing speed and special video cards. The size of the video image has traditionally been small, postage stamp or slightly bigger, although again with technological advances the ability to provide full-screen good quality video is now with us.

Types of tasks which can be used with multimedia-based digital video for language learning

This section lists some of the ways in which digital video can be exploited for a variety of language learning purposes. These tasks can, and are, used with a TV and video, but there are several advantages to their use in the computer environment. These are:

– the video is controlled by the learners, they can pace their viewing, repeat difficult passages or parts of interest
– the video can be linked and submerged within other learning resources, e.g. subtitles, definitions, grammar explanations
– all the materials, instructions, tasks, solutions, explanations can be in one place
– learners can easily take text materials away with them through copy and paste to a floppy disc.

Comprehension tasks

Simplistically, video-based listening comprehension might be approached through a three-stage sequence of tasks (Underwood, 1989), before watching, while watching and after watching. The before watching tasks aim to raise learners' awareness and activate mental schemata about the content and language of the video. Underwood (1989: 113) lists nineteen types of paper-based tasks which can be used to accompany listening comprehension, such as questions, choices from pictures, true or false, put in order, grid filling, multiple choice, etc., all to be completed in real time whilst listening. These aim to assist the listener to extract the main messages in the text. Most of the task types that Underwood (1989) describes can be replicated in the multimedia environment and, for example, be used in multimedia worksheets (Lesson idea 1, below). The after watching tasks can either exploit further the language or the content of the video.

Presentations and projects

Digital video can be integrated into learners' own presentations and projects. This may add interest and variety to the finished presentation and involve learners in the processes of exploration, comprehension and selection of video en route. Digital video clips can easily be integrated into *Powerpoint* presentations.

Freezing the video clip

This technique involves watching a small section of video until a pre-determined frame is reached and the video stops. Learners can then work together to predict what will occur next, to compose the continuation of the dialogue or to decide what they would like to know from the next sequence of video. Any of these can then be compared with the original. Alternatively, the video may be halted following a specific linguistic feature which the author considers to be useful: this could be a function, grammatical pattern, or an intonation or pronunciation feature. Video is thus used to contextualise and illustrate the language item.

Information gaps with sound only or with sound and image

These involve learners working with the video in pairs and can be used for listening and speaking work. One learner watches the video image with the sound and the other looks away or closes her eyes. The learner without access to the video image tries to imagine what is happening, and when the clip finishes she describes what she believes occurred on-screen. The learner who has watched the video then confirms or corrects after which they both then watch with sound and picture.

Jigsaw viewing

This involves dividing a video clip into five or more parts. Each of these individual clips is watched and the learner makes a decision about their order as in the original sequence. The division needs to be done judiciously so that there are no very obvious clues as to the sequence from the video image. Editing digital video is much easier than editing video tape. This task provides an opportunity for listening work and success will usually depend on correct interpretation of discourse markers.

Video with subtitles

The gains in comprehension attributed to the use of subtitled-video were documented above. Most commercial EFL CD-ROMs provide video with English subtitles together with the option to view with or without these subtitles. Where available, video could be watched without sound or subtitles while learners note down the dialogue or phrases which they believe are used and these can be checked with sound and subtitles. If used in the multimedia worksheets idea below (Lesson idea 1), then three different sets of subtitles could be provided and learners choose which is the correct set. In tasks which follow comprehension work, access to subtitles can be used to unlock language which may be lost in fast speech, and therefore allow learners to follow up on any new phrases and vocabulary.

Picture only

There are a variety of uses of the video image without the sound. This might be used as a pre-comprehension activity with learners watching and speculating about the content, e.g. participants' jobs, class, accent, motives, feelings. This prepares viewers for the version with sound. Learners might be asked to watch and provide their own versions of the dialogue and then compare them with the original. It might be used to provide input for creative writing or as scene setting for reading texts.

Lesson ideas for digital video in EFL

These lesson ideas provide ideas about some of the different ways in which computer-based digital video can be used. Teachers can take these ideas and adapt them through the inclusion of different video sources or different tasks, to provide materials which aim to develop listening skills or strategies of learners with different needs at different levels.

Lesson idea 1: Multimedia worksheets

This idea shows how multimedia worksheets which combine video, sound, pictures, and text can be created without any specialist programming knowledge. Teachers generally do not have such skills, nor the time to acquire them. Many, though, are able to use word processors such as *Word 2* (Microsoft). Modern word processors are sophisticated in that they also allow video, sound, animations, and pictures to function within a word-processed document. Thus the word-processor can be used to create multimedia language learning worksheets. These save expenditure on multiple copies of CD-ROMs, can be used in self-access or whole class mode, and enable learners to go at their own pace through language learning materials. A more detailed account of such worksheets can be found in Brett (1997).

Computer requirements

- A word processor – *Word 2* or above
- Video or sound files from the sources mentioned above, preloaded onto the hard disc of the computer
- A floppy disc on which to save the worksheets and their answer sheets

Preparation

- In a *Word* file prepare a sequence of learning tasks which are relevant to the level, interests and needs of the learners. Use a lot of white space. The file needs to be locked so as to prevent learners accidentally changing the learning material, and so that they can be reused by other learners. You lock a *Word* document by giving it a password when you save it – or alternatively use the back-up file which will have the extension .bak.
- In a separate *Word* file prepare the answers and explanations to the tasks, plus references to further sources of information, learning strategies advice, recommendations for further work, etc. Learners can then open the answer document and use it in tandem with the worksheet.
- If you only have one copy of a CD-ROM from which you have used source material such as video or audio files, then copy these files from the CD-ROM on to the hard disc of each computer. Please make sure though that you are not infringing copyright and acknowledge all the sources.
- To insert video files into a Word document choose 'Insert' → 'Object' then choose the type of 'Object', e.g. *Media clip* → and then its source, e.g. C:\Worksheet\Mafia.mov. *MediaPlayer* then allows you the option of allowing the video clip to be named and to have a play bar on it so that learners can stop, start and rewind the clip.

Space does not allow the complete worksheet to be shown, but Fig. 1 below shows the tasks related to the video. This worksheet was used with Upper Intermediate learners working in pairs and aimed to extend vocabulary of crime, to provide an opportunity to listen for specific information and to listen for specific language forms. It centred around a video scene from a famous film. It then focused on the different uses of *would*. The whole worksheet consisted of a series of fifteen tasks and used edutainment CDs for its picture, video, sound and text sources. Learners worked through the tasks at their own pace, checked their own answers and the teacher was free to monitor and assist when needed. The example shown uses traditional question and answer tasks with the video; however, there are many other task possibilities for digital video in such integrated skills worksheets. These include:

- Put a series of video clips into their correct order
- Use silent video clips as advance organisers
- Match soundless video to a choice of subtitles
- Ask learners to choose the correct continuation for a video clip from written choices
- Any of the 19 while-listening activities suggested by Underwood (1989: 113)
  e.g. true/false, multiple choice, predicting, putting pictures in order.

Task 6 - *Before you watch*
You are going to watch a short scene from the movie *The Godfather*. Tell a friend whether you think:

a) the Godfather (Marlon Brando) forgives the priest or
b) the priest forgives the Godfather.

Task 7
Watch the video (double click on the picture of New York below) and answer these questions (a–e):

a) Whose wedding day is it?
b) Who has been disrespectful?
c) Whose daughter has been ruined?
d) Why will the priest's enemies fear him?
e) What might the Godfather ask the priest to do for him?

Task 8 - *While watching*
Watch the video again and put these (a–e) phrases in the order that you hear them.

a) on my daughter's wedding day
b) Are you my friend?
c) and that day may never come
d) would be suffering
e) What have I ever done

Fig. 1 An example of part of a multimedia worksheet

Lesson idea 2: Self-correcting dictation with digital video

The aim of this activity is to provide self-correcting and self-paced video dictation tasks. It can be used as a self-access or as a whole class activity, with all levels of learners. Ideally use authentic video clips. The activity provides practice in the segmentation of words in continuous authentic speech and recognition of assimilations, contractions, weak forms, elision and weakly stressed words. It also raises awareness of the relationship between sound and spelling in English. It is essential though that learners are prepared before attempting the total cloze task. This might involve discussion around the topic of the clip or other tasks. Two examples are provided below, one uses the program *Fun with Texts* (Camsoft) and the other *Storyboard* (Wida).

Computer requirements
- A total cloze program such as *Fun with Texts* or *Storyboard*.
- A video clip of 1–2 minutes relevant to learners' needs and interests.
- *Media Player* if using *Fun with Texts,* or any video file in .avi format for *Storyboard.*

Preparation
- The video clip needs to be loaded on to the hard disc of the computer.
- The text of the video clip needs to be transcribed by the teacher and authored in the *Fun with Texts* or *Storyboard* package.

Pre-computer work
Learners discuss the topic, predict content of the video clip, watch the video with accompanying comprehension tasks. Teacher gives feedback on task success.

Computer work
1. Learners open *Fun with Texts* and select the appropriate file.
2. Choose 'Copywrite Hard' and then 'Start without seeing text' from the *Fun with Texts* menu.
3. Open 'Media Player' and select related video clip.
4. Learners have 15 minutes to complete the cloze using the video clip. The video clip is totally under their control and can be stopped and started. Feedback on right or wrong written entries is provided by the software.

Fig. 2 Self-correcting dictation activity using Fun with Texts *and a video clip*

Pre-computer work

In the *Storyboard* 'Introduction' section prepare a list of pre-watching discussion questions.

Computer work

1. Learners open the *Storyboard* file and first watch the video clip, here a clip called 'Job Interview' preferably accompanied by guided tasks.
2. Learners have ten minutes to complete the cloze using the video clip. The video clip is totally under their control for stopping and starting, and feedback on right/wrong written entries is provided by the software.

Fig. 3. Self-correcting dictation activity using Storyboard *and a video clip*

Lesson idea 3: Using real time video with business English students

This shows how video which is played in real time from the Internet might be used with learners. The player software *RealPlayer G7* comes already loaded with access to numerous news broadcast sites such as *CNN Headline News, Fox News, ABCNews and Bloomberg Business News,* all useful for business English learners. The software also comes with a search engine to uncover WWW sites with streamed video or audio on many topics. The advantage of using video from these sources is that it is up to the minute stuff, is usually short, and demands no technical preparation, just an Internet site from which the clips can be retrieved. In addition, as there is such a variety of these news sites, they can be used to compare the different emphases or angles put on news stories by different channels. There will be a short wait while the video clip is arriving on learners' computers and this time can be used for pre-watching activities.

Preparation
– Teacher needs to evaluate, select and familiarise herself with the content and language of the video clips to be used.
– Decide which listening skills or strategies the use of the video is to develop. Plan integration of the use of video into a coherent integrated skills lesson.

Pre-computer work

Lead-in – discussion
– What have been the main news stories recently?
– What issues have been involved?
– What is your opinion about the causes of the problems?

Computer work
Here is a list of activities that could be used with the real time video clips:
– One student watches without sound and relates what they feel to be the story to the other. Both then watch with sound and check.
– Note-taking – about the main issues.
– Different groups watch video from different news sites, take notes on the stories and then compare these with other groups in order to pick similar and different content.
– Pre-prepared tasks e.g. true/false, topics in order, multiple choice, gap-filling.
– Dictation from the clip, alone or in pairs.
– In pairs learners watch with sound, then in turn they watch without sound and provide the commentary or dialogue themselves. Finally both watch with sound again and note differences.
– Learners stop the video at a certain point and predict the language or action which is to follow. Then watch and check.

Computer follow-up work
Watch again and note down new vocabulary/language chunks. Explain what they know about the background to the story and what might happen next.

Fig. 4. An example of a lesson based on a video newsclip viewed with RealPlayer™

Lesson idea 4: Using dedicated CD-ROMs

The example on the next page shows how a dedicated business English CD-ROM might be used with an advanced class. It uses a video clip of an interview with the Chief Executive of Waterford Wedgwood and is taken from *International Sales – Waterford Wedgwood* (Philips, 1997). The approach adopted here integrates the use of the CD-ROM video material with work on other language skills. For an excellent account of the numerous ways in which all types of CD-ROMs can be used, see Sharma (1998).

Pre-computer work

1. Students come to the class having already used the WWW to research the
   a) products b) history c) turnover d) markets of Waterford Wedgwood.
2. Following a pair exchange of the information they have gathered, teacher leads
   a brainstorm of the main information.
3. Group discussion – 'If you were Chief Executive of Waterford Wedgwood what
   targets would you set for the company and how would you increase sales?'
4. Ideas from each group feedback to whole class.

Computer work

5. Learners complete the on-screen – 'Before you watch' which asks them to select
   two phrases which the Chief Executive will use from a choice of eight. Feedback
   given on-screen.
6. Learners watch the video clip interview with the Chief Executive and compare
   their ideas about targets and ways of increasing sales with his. No subtitles
   allowed.
7. Learners complete on-screen true/false tasks while watching the video.
8. Watch video with the subtitles – stop and note down new phrases or vocabulary.

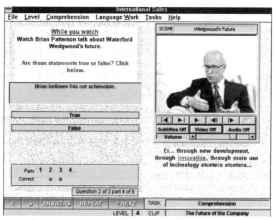

Follow-up work

9. Grammar work – ways of talking about the future.

Fig. 5 A screen shot of English for Business – International Sales *(Philips, 1998)*

References

Anderson A & T Lynch (1988) *Listening* Oxford University Press

Balatova I (1994) The impact of video on the comprehension skills of core French students *The Canadian Modern Language Review 50*

Borrás I & R C Lafayette (1994) Effects of multimedia courseware subtitling on the speaking performance of college students of French *The Modern Language Journal 78*

Brett P (1996) Using multimedia – an investigation of learners' attitudes *Computer Assisted Language Learning Journal 9*

Brett P (1997) A comparative study of the effects of the use of multimedia on listening comprehension *System 25*

Business Territory (1997) Lingonet Finland (CD-ROM)

Chapelle C A (1997) CALL in the year 2000: Still in search of research agendas? *Language Learning and Technology 1 1* http://polyglot.cal.msu.edu/llt/vol1num1/chapelle/default.html

Chapelle C A (1998) Multimedia CALL: Lessons to be learned from research on instructed SLA *Language Learning and Technology 2 1* http://llt.msu.edu/vol2num1/article1/index.html

Chun D M & J L Plass (1996) Effects of multimedia annotations on vocabulary acquisition *Modern Language Journal 80*

Cinemania (1999) Microsoft (CD-ROM)

Danan M (1992) Reversed subtitling and dual coding theory: New directions for foreign language instruction *Language Learning 42*

Dickinson L (1987) *Self Instruction in Language Learning* Cambridge University Press

Doughty C (1991a) Theoretical motivations for IVD software research and development. In Bush M, A Slaton, M Verano & M E Slayden (Eds.) *Interactive videodisc the 'why' and the 'how'*: CALICO Monograph Volume 2 Brigham Young University

Doughty C (1991b) Second language instruction does make a difference: evidence from an empirical study of SL relativisation *Studies in Second Language Acquisition 31*

Encarta 99 (1999) Microsoft (CD-ROM)

English for Business Series (1997) Philips and University of Wolverhampton (CD-ROM)

Europlus+ Reward (1998) Young Digital Poland (CD-ROM)

Fun with Texts (1997) Camsoft

Garza T J (1991) Evaluating the use of captioned video materials in advanced foreign language learning: *Foreign Language Annals 24*

Grezel J E D & A G Sciarone (1994) Computer testing of listening comprehension *Computers in Education 23*

Grimes T (1990) Audio-video correspondence and its role in attention and memory *Educational Technology Research and Development 38 3*

Guillory H G (1998) The effects of keyword captions to authentic French video on learner comprehension: *CALICO Journal 15*

Herron C, M Morris, T Secules & L Curtis (1995) A comparison of the effects of video-based versus text-based instruction in the foreign language classroom: *The French Review 68*

Herron C, P Cole, H York & P Linden (1998) A comparison study of student retention of foreign language video: Declarative versus interrogative advance organiser *The Modern Language Journal 82 2*

Interchange (1998) CD-ROM Cambridge University Press

Johnstone J & L Milne (1995) Scaffolding second language communicative discourse with teacher controlled multimedia *Foreign Language Annals 28*

Liou H C (1997) Research of on-line help as learner strategies for multimedia CALL evaluation *CALICO Journal 14*

Nunan D (1989) *Designing Tasks for the Communicative Classroom* Cambridge University Press

Porter D & J Roberts (1981) Authentic listening activities *English Language Teaching 36*

Ramsey R (1991) French in action and the grammar question *French Review 65 2*

Rost M (1990) *Listening in Language Learning* Longman

Schmidt R & S Frota (1986) Developing basic conversational ability in a second language: a case study of an adult learner of Portuguese in Day R (Ed.) *Talking to Learn: Conversation in Second Language Acquisition* Newbury House

Secules T, C Herron & M Tomessello (1992) The effect of video context on foreign language learning *The Modern Language Journal 76*

Sharma P (1998) *The CD-ROM Teachers' Handbook* Summertown Press

Sheerin S (1987) Listening comprehension: teaching or testing? *English Language Teaching Journal 78 2*

Sinclair J (1991) *Corpus, Concordance, Collocation* Oxford University Press

Storyboard (1998) Wida Software

Stokes J (1984) *Elementary Task Listening* Cambridge University Press

Teichart H U (1996) A comparative study using illustrations brainstorming and questions as advance organisers in Intermediate College German conversation classes *The Modern Language Journal 80 4*

Underwood M (1989) *Teaching Listening* Longman

4 Building bridges on the Web: Using the Internet for cultural studies

Aidan Thorne and Christine Thorne, *The British Council, Poznań, Poland*

Aidan Thorne is currently working for the British Council in Poland as coordinator of an IT in education project. He has worked as an English teacher and teacher trainer in a number of countries including Morocco, Egypt, Oman, China and Poland.

Christine Thorne has worked as an English teacher and teacher trainer in a number of countries including Morocco, Egypt, Oman and China. She currently works for the British Council in Poland where she is Senior Lecturer in Applied Linguistics at Adam Mickiewicz University in Poznań. athorne@main.amu.edu.pl

Intercultural competence as a goal

English Language teaching today seems far removed from the times when 'culture in language' meant studying 'big C' topics such as great literary works, artistic masterpieces and texts about historic events. Since the publication of Hymes' (1971) article 'On communicative competence', language and culture have been regarded as inseparable. This in turn ignited fierce methodological and philosophical debate in both English language teaching and cultural studies circles which is still ongoing and evolving. As Byram (1998: 94) points out: 'The problem with the notion of communicative competence is that it is based on a description of how native speakers speak to each other'; in today's post-communicative era the cultural and linguistic 'superiority' of the native speaker is no longer automatically assumed. W R Lee remarked:

> All of us are 'foreigners'. Let's recognise that we inhabit not merely our countries of upbringing but wider and supra-national communities and indeed 'the great globe' itself.
>
> (W R Lee, Founder Chair IATEFL Conference Speech 1992.)

There is now much debate centred on the question of whether or not English will maintain its status as a 'world language' (e.g. Graddol, 1997; Crystal, 1997) and a recognition that if this is to be the case, there is a need to develop new methodologies to train teachers and learners to take into account the fact that English has become a world resource which is no longer controlled by native speakers in the 'centre' environments and conveyed to non-native speakers in 'periphery' environments (cf. Phillipson, 1992). The challenge for language teacher training, according to Byram (ibid.), is to enable teachers to be teachers of language *and* culture, the development of 'intercultural competence' in language teachers is thus a prerequisite to enable them to develop it in their learners. Byram defines the competence of the proficient intercultural speaker in terms of a number of interrelated skills, 'partial competences' and knowledge. In addition to the linguistic, sociolinguistic and discourse skills which form one's communicative competence, the interculturally competent individual needs to possess the skills of interpreting and relating, the skills of discovery and interaction, a curiosity and openness of attitude, a knowledge of the products and practices of social groups in one's own country as well as one's interlocutor's country, and perhaps most crucially, a critical cultural awareness that enables one to evaluate critically and in an informed manner, the particular perspectives, practices and products of one's own and other cultures (Byram, 1998: 95–96). The methodological shift towards the development of intercultural competence can be observed in a variety of recent cultural studies publications which place emphasis on cross-cultural awareness, exploration, understanding and mutual tolerance and respect. For example, the Macquarie University *Handbook in Intercultural Communication* series (edited by Brick) which has volumes on China, Japan and Poland; *Crossing Cultures: British Cultural Studies for 12th Grade Romanian Students* (1998) produced by a predominantly Romanian team in collaboration with the British Council in Romania; and *Branching Out: A Cultural Studies Syllabus* (1998) produced by a mixed Bulgarian and British team in cooperation with the British Council in Bulgaria.

The growing role of technology in fostering intercultural competence

The last few years have seen a period of phenomenal growth and expansion of the Internet. From modest beginnings in the 1960s we are now witnessing, according to Crystal (1998), 'a potential technological revolution of unprecedented scope [which aims] to enable people all over the world to communicate with each other in seconds'.

If we accept this view, then the Internet surely has much to offer in the fields of cultural studies and language learning. Indeed, teachers around the world are already making use of the resources and potential offered by the Internet in a variety of ways in their work. These include sharing lesson plans, materials and ideas with other teachers participating in dedicated discussion forums; both teachers and students are using the information resources available on the Internet to research projects, assignments and materials and to make contact with peers and colleagues all over the world for the mutual exchange of ideas and opinions.

E-mail

The service most people are familiar with and certainly the most widely used of all the Internet services is electronic mail (e-mail). Like a fax, delivery is virtually immediate; a message sent to the other side of the world should take no longer than a few minutes to arrive. However, here the similarity ends. Not only is e-mail cheaper as it involves just the price of a local phone call, but it also allows you to send a message simultaneously to any number of people by simply adding their addresses to the list. Speed and coverage of delivery are not the only advantages of e-mail. Messages can include attachments such as word-processed documents, sound, graphics and (very short) video files which can be sent at the same time. This makes it a very powerful medium for sharing and exchanging information quickly and at a distance. It also provides a platform for setting up and managing cross-cultural projects. There are many of these already in operation; a good example of the type of project that can be set up is the recent ELTeCS *Future of English* course and follow up 'virtual workshop' coordinated by The English Company and the British Council.

Other examples and information about e-mail projects may be found at the *Windows on the World* website http://www.wotw.org.uk which was set up to act as a kind of junction box aimed at helping schools at all levels find cross-cultural project partners around Europe.

Newsgroups

A second, potentially very useful, Internet resource is the system of newsgroups. There are thousands of different newsgroups dealing with every conceivable subject in a wide variety of languages (although predominantly English at the moment). Forums like these, providing they are not abused, are valuable venues for posing questions and getting answers, sharing ideas and enabling people to communicate across borders and continents, thus allowing intercultural communication in a virtual setting.

World Wide Web (WWW)

Thirdly, there is the World Wide Web (the Web). In essence this is the combined information resources of all the computer locations around the world which have made their data freely available. Web pages may include animations, sound or video, in addition to text.

The wealth of information on the Web means that by exploiting the resources, learners can engage in both short- and long-term 'discovery' learning tasks and projects, thus expanding their knowledge and developing the interactive and operational skills demanded for the development of intercultural competence (see above). Excellent examples of the type of activities and projects that can be set up, and a rationale for the approach may be found on the 'WebQuest' site at http://edweb.sdsu.edu/webquest/webquest.html/

Other examples of cross-cultural projects include the 'Space Knowledge Adventure' project presented by Coolderry Central school in Ireland, aimed at linking students in 200 primary schools throughout Europe (http://www.theguardians.com) and the 'Do you talk Internet?' project based in Belgium and aimed at promoting Internet multilingualism (http://www.darespeak.org).

Teachers wanting to use the Web with their learners need to exercise caution. Internet content must also be regarded with caution. Crystal (1998) outlines a number of points that need to be borne in mind when looking for material:

- Quality is often inconsistent and there is no advance way of distinguishing between what is good/relevant versus what is bad/irrelevant.
- While the information on the Web is impressive in its range it may be unsystematic. In a nutshell: whether you find information on a particular topic depends entirely on whether someone has bothered to set pages up in the first place.
- Pages are often not updated to ensure they remain contemporary or even relevant.

The filtering and control normally exercised by the publishing industry is largely absent on the Web, thus it is vital that any individual using it adopts a critical approach to the information they find there (see David Eastment's article from *MET* on http://www.eastment.com).

It could be claimed therefore, that the democratic nature of the Web, far from being problematic, in fact represents an ideal environment to practise and acquire the skills of interpretation, evaluation, discovery, interaction and critical awareness which Byram (ibid.) maintains are vital for the development of intercultural competence.

A case study in website development: the British Studies website in Poland

The rest of this chapter will explore the construction of a specific website that will illustrate what you might do if you wanted to set up something similar. It will not go into the technical details about design and development, but will talk about the stages that were gone through, showing the motivations for developing the pages and some of the materials.

Given the rapidly expanding use of technology for educational purposes, the British Council in Poland were keen to look at ways in which they could usefully exploit this exciting potential. Initial discussions about the feasibility of developing a website were encouraging, and market research indicated interest from teachers and educational institutions within Poland. The planning of the site began in September 1997 and centred around a number of questions, including: Why develop a website instead of using a more traditional means of delivery? Is such a technology-based resource feasible and sustainable in the Polish context? What design constraints would need to be taken into account within the local context? What should be on the site? These questions will be the focus of the remainder of this article and similar questions should be asked by you before you think about a similar undertaking, even if it is going to be a small site.

Why develop a website?

Prior to the early 1990s, the language teaching focus in Poland was on languages other than English. However, in the relatively short period since that time, the growth in numbers of students and teachers involved in ELT has increased dramatically. To date there are approximately 8 million students in the Polish school system, of whom nearly 4 million are studying English, with nearly 18,000 qualified teachers catering to their needs. Obviously this has led to an increased interest in finding out about English-speaking cultures and equally obviously, teachers of English want to be able to satisfy this interest. At the same time Poles are keen to participate in the wider community and share information about themselves; one Polish teacher commenting on the opportunities for contact and exchange which have become available in the post-communist era says:

> it is the sense of belonging to a very active and intellectually lively professional community – in my country, the region, and world-wide – which has not only stimulated but empowered me to try and achieve even more far-reaching development. (The British Council, 1996: 7)

A website therefore seemed to provide the ideal vehicle to cater for these various needs. The fact that the use of the Web in Poland is still (relatively) in its infancy with most local sites focussing on advertising rather than content was nevertheless an issue that could not be ignored. Despite this, it was generally felt that it can only be a matter of time before institutions and individuals start to develop the different ways in which they use the medium (indeed this is already happening, see below).

Economic factors were also involved in the decision to follow the electronic route. Hard copy resources had been made available by the British Council at a series of British Studies Resource Points throughout Poland, but it soon became obvious that demand was outstripping supply and the updating and developing of these Points would be beyond the resources of any donor agency. It was decided that web-based materials represented a cost-effective alternative. Although development costs for both traditional hard-copy and web-based materials are arguably the same – after all, someone has to write them! – the ongoing development and updating of materials based on a website is considerably easier, faster and cheaper to deal with. If it is necessary to make changes to the site, it is simply a case of opening the relevant file(s) on the server and adding to them or deleting where necessary. This sidesteps delays that may be created by time-consuming negotiations about costs and print schedules with publishers and printers. Moreover, as the delivery of web-based materials from the site to the user involves only the cost of a local phone call, it is potentially a much faster and cheaper mode of delivery than distributing hard-copy materials to resources points by air, road and rail links. Using a website as a storage and delivery point has the added attraction that it can be open 24 hours a day and requires no staff on-site to operate it or deal with customers.

Is it sustainable?

In his 1996 report *ELT and the Internet in Poland*, commissioned by the British Council, David Eastment paints a fairly bleak picture of the IT presence in Poland. Eastment reported the existence of only 40 Internet Service Providers and approximately 15,000 Internet hosts nationwide. However, by the time the BS web project was in its early stages of development this picture was already beginning to change, and what is more, beginning to change at a rapid pace. For example, Internet access and the possibility of e-mail accounts has been freely available in many universities for some time. A recent survey (Mizgajska, 1998) of 100 in-service teachers studying extra-murally at Adam Mickiewicz University in Poznań, revealed that all the respondents were aware of what the Internet is, and 95% were interested in using the Internet as a resource for professional development. 57% reported that they already make use of computer technology in some form in their teaching. Just three years after Eastment's initial report, developments in the IT arena in Poland are staggering. In common with other countries, equipment costs are falling all the time and the number of ISPs has now risen from 40 to over 240 with a parallel rise in the numbers of hosts in institutions. This represents an increase of some 600%. Information gathered from the Internet for Schools project (Internet dla Skol – IDS – http://www.ids.com.pl) shows that more than 600 schools in Poland are developing their own websites, which in some cases are very elaborate and technologically sophisticated.

The indications are clear: access to the WWW by Polish institutions across the educational spectrum is on the increase, and teachers and educators are quite obviously exploring the possibilities of harnessing new and existing technologies for educational purposes. Thus the British Council was optimistic about the sustainability of the venture.

Design constraints

Although the assessment of the general picture of IT development in education in Poland is a positive one, it was nevertheless decided to err on the side of caution in terms of site design; the reasoning behind this was to make the site as attractive as possible to as broad a spectrum of people as possible. In designing the site, the team were conscious of a number of technical design constraints. These included:

– The type of connection – permanent, freely available and fast access via a workplace vs modem/PC.
– Variable connection quality in different regions.
– Varied types of equipment available in primary/secondary schools (a major part of the target audience).
– The site needed to follow the standardised format of the main British Council (BC) site and use standard BC banners, logos and buttons. (In the event this did not prove to be disadvantageous, as the main BC interface is easy to use and fitted the above criteria, in other words there are no frames and few inbuilt 'bells and whistles' that might slow access.)

In order to cope with these technical and design constraints it was decided to limit what was put into the materials in various ways. To summarise, the team:

– Limited the use of graphics in the design of the interface (few icons) to help speed of access.
– Opted for technology like *Javascript*[1] rather than using a multimedia approach (sound, video).
– Refrained from using frames wherever possible to speed up access.
– Selected/commissioned simple graphics with low colour density, variety and clear outlines (line drawings) to illustrate site materials.
– Took into consideration different colour and monitor resolutions so that what graphics were used were useful enhancements to the materials rather than time wasters.
– Ensured that all materials were readable by a wide variety of browsers including *Internet Explorer* and *Netscape* as well as the older Unix text-only browsers like *Lynx*.

Bearing in mind the points above, the overall aim was to produce a site with materials which looked good and were usable online, using the resources available on the Web, but which could also be printed out and used in a scaled down form (i.e. without the possibilities offered by hyperlinks) so that teachers could exploit them as a hard copy resource in class. In practice the pages look very attractive on colour print outs and reasonably good when printed in black and white format, thus ensuring their availability across printer platforms from laser jet down to low quality dot matrix printers.

These issues are an important decision before you start making materials. You need to know who your audience is going to be and what sort of technology and technological skills they have, in order to make informed decisions about how to proceed.

What is on the site?

The site is essentially a storehouse of regularly updated, themed teaching materials, many of them original items produced by local teachers and students. To date, areas covered have been Views of Britain, Contemporary British Festivals, Youth Culture and Fashion, Education and Government. Other topics planned for the future include Sport and Health.

Each edition contains a number of types of teaching materials including:

– Texts and articles in English from both native and non-native speaker sources with suggested discussion questions and, where relevant, tasks. The intention with these is to provide teachers with a basic resource they can adapt and develop for themselves.
– Whole lesson plans including teachers' notes.
– Extracts from British Studies related coursebooks.
– A regularly updated bibliography of hard-copy and electronic cultural studies resources. Later editions include an annotated bibliography of coursebook references relevant to the theme being covered but limited to those coursebooks available in regional resource points (see above).
– Links to interesting websites with a cultural/cross-cultural theme where teachers and students may find extra materials and resources.

Plans for the future

It is hoped that the site can eventually be linked up to other related sites based in Poland and beyond as part of a network of cultural studies forums. The process of archiving back issues of the site and making them available in hard copy at the network of British Council British Studies resource points has already begun, thus increasing availability of the materials. A CD-ROM version of the site is now available.

Feedback about the site regularly comes in from within Poland and beyond; the majority of hits have been from Poland but there have also been callers from as far afield as Japan and Mexico. Great potential exists for developing a series of interlinked websites where teachers and students can go to find materials, ask questions and share answers and experiences with other people from different backgrounds and nationalities.

As the Polish experience shows, the Web can be a useful, cost-effective and exciting means of providing teachers and students with supplementary resources and information, building bridges across cultures.

The website can be accessed at: http://elt.britcoun.org.pl

A look at the site

Since the site aims at being a forum for cultural exploration, the materials and tasks it contains aim to develop the notion of intercultural competence. Tomalin and Stempelski

66

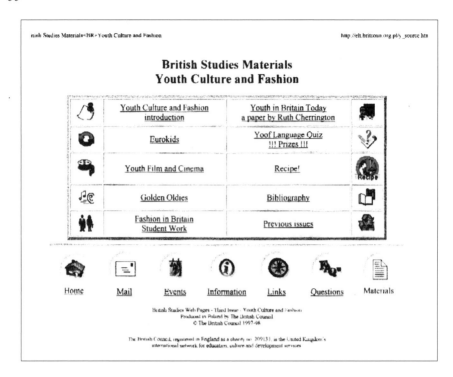

British Studies Materials
Youth Culture and Fashion

	Youth Culture and Fashion introduction	Youth in Britain Today a paper by Ruth Cherrington	
	Eurokids	Yoof Language Quiz !!! Prizes !!!	
	Youth Film and Cinema	Recipe!	
	Golden Oldies	Bibliography	
	Fashion in Britain Student Work	Previous issues	

Home Mail Events Information Links Questions Materials

British Studies Web Pages - Third Issue - Youth Culture and Fashion
Produced in Poland by The British Council
© The British Council 1997-98

The British Council, registered in England as a charity no. 209131, is the United Kingdom's
international network for education, culture and development services

(1993: 7–8) offer a modified version of Seelye's (1988) framework for facilitating the development of cross-cultural communication skills. Many of the principles they include in their list of 'goals of cultural instruction' have been used as design criteria for the teaching materials and tasks on the site.

Sample materials 1

The lesson plan that follows, for example, aims to help learners develop an understanding of the fact that all people exhibit culturally conditioned behaviours (Tomalin and Stempelski's first goal). It also helps students to develop the ability to refine generalisations about the target culture, in terms of supporting evidence (Tomalin and Stempelski's fifth goal) and it increases their awareness of the cultural connotations of words and phrases in the target language (Tomalin and Stempelski's fourth goal). At each stage of the lesson reference is made not only to the target culture, but also to the students' own culture. Scheu (1997) remarks that 'in studying another culture, the learner will and must learn about himself in the process' thus, to achieve cross-cultural understanding and mutual tolerance, an awareness of one's own culturally conditioned behaviours and values is as vital as an understanding of those of the target culture (see Seelye, 1988, for a discussion of the concept of cultural relativity).

FOR THE TEACHER

A classroom activity

What do you think the British are really like? How different are they from Polish people? What do your students think? Are you interested in exploring these issues further in class? If so, the session below could help you. Basic guidelines and teachers' notes have been included although individual teachers may wish to adapt them to suit their needs.

Topic: Views of Britain
Level: Intermediate to Advanced
Time: Approximately one hour
Materials: Blackboard and a piece of paper for each student
Aims:
– To promote classroom discussion
– To develop an awareness of cross-cultural issues and attitudes

Stage 1
Give out copies of the chart that follows or get the students to copy it from the board.

Column A	Column B
Punctual	Always late

– Ask the students in pairs or groups to fill in Column A with seven words or short phrases that in their opinion describe the British (see example). Then ask them to consider where these ideas come from (e.g. TV, books, parents).
– Get students to fill in Column B with the opposite words or phrases (see example).
– Get students to look at each other's lists to find similarities and differences.

Stage 2
– Which of these characteristics are positive or negative? Get students in pairs/groups to indicate their opinions with a minus (–) for negative characteristics and a plus (+) for positive characteristics. Get them to take notes of their reasons.

– Get them to link each pair of words with a line, discuss where they feel Polish people would fall on the line and make a mark to indicate this. Get them to take notes of their reasons.

– Get them to look at other groups' ideas and find similarities and differences.

– Hold a feedback session to bring these out.

Stage 3

– So far the discussion has revolved around societies in terms of people. However, cultures and societies do not only differ in terms of 'national characteristics'; there may also be great variety amongst different cultures in the way we perceive the world around us.

– The next activity uses the learners' first language as well as English to explore cultural variation in typical aspects of daily life. The teacher can choose which lexical items to focus on: the chart below is just an example.

English word	Polish word	Similarities of meaning	Differences of meaning
lunch			
wedding			
housing estate			
holidays			

Students should work together to complete the chart. For each word they should try to think of ways in which the meaning of the item is similar in Polish and ways in which it may be different. For example, according to *Longman Dictionary of English Language and Culture Lunch* is 'a usu. light meal eaten in the middle of the day' (p. 791). In what ways is this similar to Polish eating habits? In what ways is it different?

Students may not necessarily know the 'correct' answer but they should try to guess based on their knowledge of Polish and British culture. They should be encouraged to look in dictionaries and other reference books to support their answers. The session can conclude with a discussion of what learners have discovered about similarities and differences.

Sample materials 2

The materials below (The Changing Face of Britain) focus on the diversity of contemporary Britain and its population. The tasks are intended to stimulate students' intellectual curiosity about the target culture, and encourage empathy towards its peoples (Tomalin and Stempelski's seventh goal). The subject matter is also intended to combat stereotypical views of Britain and Britishness. The inclusion of hyperlinks encourages students to explore the resources of the Web, and the questions and tasks encourage students to relate what they learn to their own culture (Byram's discovery of new cultural knowledge, interpretation and relation of it to one's own culture).

Laksmi Divali (Festival of Light)
There is a significantly large Hindu population in Britain and Divali, or the Festival of Light, held in honour of the Hindu goddess of prosperity 'Laksmi' is their New Year festival. It is generally celebrated in the autumn between October and November. Homes are cleaned thoroughly on the day of the festival and as dusk falls lamps and candles are lit in every room of the house and outside in the front porch and garden. Then, weather permitting, the doors and windows are opened to let in the goddess to bless the house and its inhabitants. The lights are also used to scare away Alaksmi, the goddess of misfortune. People may also smash a statue of her to indicate that she is not welcome in the home. Other rituals that are observed include the cooking and eating of a family feast. Food seems to play in all festivals, irrespective of culture'

Tasks   Links

Ramadan
Islam is the second largest religion in Britain and Ramadan is one of the major festivals

The Changing Face of Britain

Sample materials 3

The tasks which accompany the essay below are designed to help learners understand that social variables such as age, sex, social class and place of residence may influence the ways in which people speak and behave (Tomalin and Stempelski's second goal). The material is also intended to stimulate discussion about similarities and differences between cultures and to emphasise that not all teaching about culture implies behaviour change, but merely an awareness and tolerance of the cultural influences affecting one's own and others' behaviour (Tomalin & Stempelski).

Malwina

I think everyone remembers their first day at school. Frightened but at the same time excited and curious seven-year-olds are glued to their mother's side. There is slight chaos and confusion among those members of the family present, who unwillingly leave behind their 'pride and joy'. My first day was almost the same. The most terrified person was my mum. I was close to tears. A typical first day at school, well it would be if this scene had taken place in my country of birth, which is Poland, but actually it took place in Great Britain, almost 20 years ago. The school assembly hall was filled with laughing and singing kids. I was too scared to say anything to my mum, who held me so close that I could hardly breathe. From that hall, which was a gathering place for all teachers, parents and kids, each school-day began with a morning prayer and a cheerful song. I loved those early mornings. I know my mother did because as each day passed from a face full of tears she could gradually see a smiling one. She could see me desperately wanting to sing one of those joyous songs and eventually I did.

It seems a life time ago, but for me it was a time I will never forget because it changed my life completely. I was a fortunate kid. Not everyone was allowed to leave Poland in the 70's. To this day I often wonder how my life would have been different if I hadn't gone to England. But, it is very difficult for me to even imagine. Children, unlike adults, have this fantastic ability to 'mix and mingle' without any inhibitions. They don't even need to use words to get their message across. Language is no barrier for them. This was how I functioned for the first couple of months. As far as I was told by my mother I was 'silent' until one day I just began to speak, a language which I had listened to and literally 'absorbed'. As a teacher now myself I know that this is how children learn. There are no language barriers for them, that is why teaching children for me has always been a pleasure. The five years I lived in England enabled me to speak the language in its natural environment and that is an advantage for me as an English teacher, but being a child I accepted what I heard without even thinking about it, that is why my first problems appeared when I decided to study English in Poland. A very bizarre situation occurred. I had to learn the language from the beginning. I had to learn to understand my spoken English. It may seem funny but I felt like I was learning the language backwards. When I became a teacher I taught children and adults, and I also taught myself how to explain things which for me were natural.

Although I came back to Poland 15 years ago, and during this time I haven't returned to England, some people still mistake me for a foreigner. For me that is not only a compliment but an acknowledgement that what you acquire as a child, no matter if it's a language, skill or an ability, can never be forgotten.

Malwina Staszak now works in a school in Warsaw

Suggested discussion questions and tasks

– What do you think Malwina means when she says she felt she was 'learning the language backwards'?
– In what ways does your knowledge of English differ from that of a native speaker?
– The table below compares some of the advantages and disadvantages of having a Polish teacher of English or a native speaker. Copy it and brainstorm some more ideas.

Advantages	Polish teacher of English	Native speaker teacher of English
	Can explain difficulties in students' mother tongue if necessary	May have up to date knowledge e.g. of slang vocabulary
	Can understand particular problems of Polish learners	As a foreigner may have understanding of how it feels to be a learner
	Usually has well developed analytical ability	May have good intuitive knowledge of language

Disadvantages	Polish teacher of English	Native speaker teacher of English
	May not know latest slang vocabulary	May not 'know' grammar

Note
[1] Javascript is a programming language for web pages that embeds its code within HTML i.e. the building block of the web.

References
BBC (1998) *Computers Don't Bite Teachers* BBC Publications

The British Council (1998) *Branching Out: A Cultural Studies Syllabus* The British Council

The British Council (1996) *Voices from the New Democracies* The British Council

Brick J (General Editor) (1995) *Handbook in Intercultural Communication* series. National Centre for English Language Teaching and Research Macquarie University

Byram M (1998) Intercultural Communicative Competence – The Challenge for Language Teacher Training in *Teaching Towards Intercultural Competence: Conference Proceedings: Sofia 1997* Cherrington & Davcheva (Eds.): 92–103 The British Council Bulgaria

Cichirdan A et al. (1998) *Crossing Cultures: British Cultural Studies for 12th Grade Romanian Students* The British Council Romania

Crystal D (1997) *English as a Global Language* Cambridge University Press

Crystal D (1998) To surf or not to surf: that is the question *Network 1/1* Poland Omnibus in association with The British Council Poland

Eastment D (1996) *ELT and the Internet in Poland* Unpublished British Council report

Graddol D (1997) *The Future of English?* The British Council London

Hymes D (1971) On communicative competence in Pride J & J Holmes (Eds.) (1972) *Sociolinguistics* Penguin

Mizgajska A (1998) *The Internet as a Resource for EFL Teacher Development*: Unpublished Magister dissertation Poznań Adam Mickiewicz University

Phillipson R (1992) *Linguistic Imperialism* Oxford University Press

Scheu: U D (1997) Towards Intercultural Education in Europe *Studia Anglica Posnaniensa* XXXII

Seelye, H N (1998) *Teaching Culture* Lincolnwood, Il National Textbook Company

Tomalin B & S Stempelski (1993) *Cultural Awareness* Oxford University Press

Acknowledgements

All materials and screen shots from the British Studies website have been reproduced by kind permission of the British Council Warsaw. Many people have been involved in the development of the website described in this article and it is not possible to mention everyone individually. However, we would like to particularly thank the following who provided us with ideas and/or materials for this article: Louise Cowcher, Wojciech Korput, Susan Maingay, Simon Smith, Malwina Staszak.

5 Communicating with computers

Gary Motteram

Gary works for Manchester University in the Centre for English Language Studies in Education and is currently the Centre Director. He is programme director for MEd courses that are to do with technology and language learning and also supervises people doing PhDs in the same topic area. Much of the work he does now is distance education.

He has been involved in IATEFL for over ten years, has been a committee member of the Computer SIG and its co-ordinator. He then became the chair of the SIG Committee and currently manages IATEFL's website. He has been involved in running a range of events as part of the Computer SIG over a number of years and until very recently was the newsletter editor.   gary.motteram@man.ac.uk

This chapter is going to focus on the way that spoken language can be promoted using computers. It is going to look at this idea from two different angles: the first being the incidental language that is generated as a part of tasks when learners work together; the second will consider the role of the computer as mediator of communication and will look at a range of technologies from the more common e-mail exchange to the increasingly available desktop videoconferencing, or Internet telephone systems.

Using computers to develop spoken language

Pennington (1989: 100) makes a long and detailed claim about the role of computers in the promotion of spoken language skills:

> The utility of computers in the oral language curriculum is in fact no less natural, and no less significant, than in the text-based curriculum. Like other media such as audiotape recordings or books, computers have two broad ways of providing instruction in speaking and listening: (1) they can create environments which facilitate interaction, and (2) they can provide training in production and perception of speech. Also like various other media, computers offer opportunities for conducting research and for testing student performance in the speech-based aspects of the language curriculum. Some of the roles of computers in language instruction are similar to those played by traditional media and may not represent advances over those media; some roles offer definite improvements over traditional ways of providing instruction; still others could not be realised at all by means of traditional media.

These are big claims and now, in addition, further claims are made about how computers allow 'real' interaction through, for example, e-mail communication. In her article Pennington (1989) goes on to describe a range of activities that have now been tried and tested in various pieces of research since she first made those statements. Much of the evidence for what Pennington in 1989 was arguing was and still is hearsay. However, a consideration of the literature might lead you to believe that an adventure game, simulation, word processing exercise, grammar game or information-gap activity is more likely than text reconstruction or vocabulary activities to promote language; this partly depends on what kind of language you are trying to promote.

Before we take this further let me describe for you a typical adventure game (albeit an old one). In a typical adventure game there are usually problems to solve, you are usually moving around in a virtual 'world' collecting objects of various types as you go and using these objects to help you solve problems. The program usually has an end result in the sense that you, eventually, win the game when you have completed a range of tasks and reached the goals that the program has set for you. These games can be long and complicated, taking several months to complete, or else they can be quite short and focus in on one fairly small area. They have been written for young children in an educational context e.g. *Granny's Garden*, for older children, e.g. *The Hobbit*, or for adults, e.g. *Sim City,* or *Riven*. Jones and Fortescue (1987: 70) quote a typical 'conversation' that would be typed in at the computer for a traditional game that has few graphics and relies heavily on text. Games have changed the way they look, with 3-D graphics, sound, animation, video and much more complex scenarios. There is often less language interaction on screen, because of the point and click environment we now inhabit, but what they do is much the same and the on screen language has been replaced by help books, websites and discussion groups where other language skills need to be used.

This possible human/computer dialogue comes from an adventure game called *The Wizard and the Princess* (Jones and Fortescue, 1987: 70). A is the human and B is the computer. On the screen are the lines of text, the rattlesnake and the rock.

A: GO NORTH

B: THE RATTLE SNAKE WON'T LET YOU GO NORTH

A: KILL SNAKE

B: WITH WHAT?

A: THROW KNIFE

B: YOUR KNIFE IS NOT BIG ENOUGH TO KILL THIS SNAKE

A: THROW ROCK

B: YOU AREN'T CARRYING IT

A: TAKE ROCK

B: THE ROCK IS MUCH TOO BIG

A: GO NORTH

B: THE RATTLESNAKE WON'T LET YOU GO NORTH ...

The main drawback with this type of game for ELT is their length and how to maintain interest. This is much easier in a general learning context: for example, in a primary school, where a lot more work can be got out of such games, so along with language work, there is potential for mathematics, drawing, history, geography and so on depending on the nature of the game itself. Straker (1989), Straker and Govier (1997) and McFarlane (1997) have written books on using computers with young children and people who work with young learners might find these helpful.

The earliest kind of adventure game came on disk, but now they mainly come on CD, or are part of the Internet. One of the older CD-ROMs that has purportedly successfully been used for language learning is *Where in the World is Carmen San Diego* (and variations on this theme). This one is certainly sold as being useful for language development. It is based around the searching analogy of the software described above and involves the learners looking for the elusive Carmen San Diego. Interestingly there is a spin-off cartoon series that makes use of the same basic ideas and it has occurred to me that the software and the video could be used in tandem. However, no reports of its use have ever appeared in the academic press.

An alternative way of using adventure games in the classroom is to use something commercial that has been specifically written for language learning, or to write one yourself. This latter prospect is not as difficult as it may seem. There are at least two commercially available adventure games that have been written specifically for the language classroom. The earliest one is disk-based and is called *London Adventure*, the most recent one is called *Oscar Lake*. The basic problem with all these types of programs is putting them in a context that the learners can understand. In fact, it is the work that goes on around the program itself that is probably the most useful language development and this is a point that we will return to when we talk about incidental language.

Research into the use of adventure games is as scarce as research into any other area of computing in the language classroom, apart perhaps from writing. However, Harrison and Cheung (1992) report positively about a specific adventure. Their research involved using an 'interactive text-only adventure game' called *Colossal Adventure*. The experiment was set up using a classic empirical model using control and treatment groups. The students were tested for specific language points related to the program and also asked about their attitudes towards using the software. The students learned the vocabulary of the game well, which implies perhaps that if adventure games were written with specific target vocabulary in mind then the learners might learn it. They were also tested for specific grammatical points that were part of the game, e.g. prepositions. Their knowledge of these items had not changed by the end of the treatment. The reactions with regard to attitudes were as follows:

subjects found the game interesting, difficult, enlightening and enjoyable. They thought they used the target language quite frequently while they were working on the game. They even considered the time they spent on the game, i.e. the eight hours in the experiment, worthwhile. Moreover, they were willing to spend more time on it. (Harrison and Cheung, 1992: 171)

A very positive outcome, but admittedly only one research article. We will look at some similar research in relation to simulations.

Simulations

There is a narrow line drawn between adventure games and simulations, but generally most ELT teachers would be familiar with the concept of simulation from other areas of their teaching, see for example Ken Jones' (1982) work in this area. Simulations are seen generally as a good way of promoting spoken language; they also attempt to model real life and may include an element of role playing depending on who the participants are. As Glyn Jones (1986: 179) says:

> I take 'simulation' to mean any learning activity which seeks to model some aspect of 'real-life' target behaviour in some way. As a learning technique it is widely used outside language teaching, and has been in use long before computers were invented. What computers have brought to the technique are their ability to model complex mathematical systems in real time (so that you do not have to calculate the likely results of your actions; the computer does it for you), and, secondly, their consequent capacity to give feedback.

Two that have been discussed in the literature are *Yellow River Kingdom* and *Fast Food*. The first one is well known because of Glyn Jones' article about his use of the program, the second one forms part of the British Council/CUP's suite of programs originally written for the BBC microcomputer and part of the first attempt at an integrated package of products for ELT. Phillips' (1987) rationale was one of the first real attempts to put together an overview of what people felt about computers in the language classroom, particularly with reference to a group of pieces of software. What he said then still makes a lot of sense now. See Legenhausen and Wolff (1988) and Jones, F (1991) for further discussion on the issue of simulations. The basic points made by all these writers and which can still be echoed is summarised by Jones, G (1986: 186) 'that the value of a computer simulation for communicative language teaching does not lie in the program itself. As with any other piece of teaching material, it depends on what you do with it!'

More recently there has been a growth in the number of simulations developed on the Web. If you are at all interested in English for Science and Technology (EST) (although at least two of these simulations could be used for general language work), you might like to have a look at the following two web addresses: http://zebu.uoregon.edu/nsf/work.html and http://zebu.uoregon.edu/nsf/cannon.html

Simulations like these are particularly useful if you work in a language support situation in schools where English might be the medium of instruction, because they integrate so well into other curriculum areas, but they are equally useful in the general EFL context. One of these simulations is concerned with use of electricity in the home and the main aim of such scenarios would be to encourage small groups of learners to talk about what is happening in the simulation and their decision-making process, and to record their ideas on a work sheet. They would then talk or write about what they have done. They may do this talking together in a lab or self–access centre, or exchange ideas via e-mail or through real-time communication.

This is the worksheet they would use to record their ideas:

CALCULATING THE COST OF YOUR YEARLY ENERGY BILL

This exercise is based on a simulation you can find at: http://zebu.uoregon.edu/nsf/work.html

It takes a while to download.

This material is based on what is called a Java applet and will help you calculate your electric energy bill.

You can select different kinds of appliances and choose how many hours a week to run them. By inputting your utility rate, your annual electric bill can be determined.

In order for it to be more useful for language learning, you will need to keep a record of what happens. Use the following table:

Appliance	Power rating in kilowatts	Cost per year

Total cost for the year = £

Material designed and developed by the author

Another simple scientific simulation is: Java Canon: http://zebu.uoregon.edu/nsf/cannon.html

With this one the students need to keep a record of the different parameters and how they affect the passage of the cannonball. This is much more technically oriented, but the principles for creating a good lesson are the same.

What is a simulation?

Let us now consider simulations in a little more detail. All of the simulations mentioned so far are what are called *move-based* as opposed to *real-time* simulations (Harrison and Cheung, 1992: 156). The principal difference between these two types of simulations is the amount of time you take. In a move-based simulation time is not critical and learners can spend as long as they like pondering their next answer. In some ways the longer the learners argue and debate the better because it promotes more incidental language use. An analogue of a real-time simulation might be the current craze for *Furbies* which die, like real animals, if you do not care for them in an effective and timely manner.

Fast Food and programs like it are move-based. These in many ways make them easier to use in a class (but see below). Let's look at Phillips' (1987: 61) description of this program:

> In FAST FOOD students have to run a fast food stall at an exhibition. This involves making decisions about the quantities of ingredients to be bought, the product mix to be offered and the prices to be charged. Basically, the stall sells hot-dogs, hamburgers, cola and coffee. The object of the exercise is to make as large a profit as possible, starting with an initial capital of £50. The simulation models six days of trading activity; in other words, it is assumed that the exhibition lasts a week.

As you might expect from the comments already made, in order to get the most out of this or any simulation you will need to do a lot of preparation with the learners in advance, as advised by Jones, G (1986). Among the many tasks possible with this simulation is the use of role play in order to practise different language registers. The print material that comes with all the British Council/CUP software certainly helps to keep a running total of what happens as you progress through the simulation, but introductory and follow up work are going to make the activity more effective.

If you would like to read about *Kingdom* then look in Jones and Fortescue (1987: 64–66), or in Jones G (1986: passim).

Simulations have not figured a great deal in the recent ELT literature despite their popularity in other walks of life. The most interesting recent article is by Francis Jones (1991). This describes a news simulation based on a very simple self-produced piece of software. This program acts as a teletyping system as learners are involved in the production of a newspaper. The teacher simply changes the datasets making using of that day's news and at random intervals the program adds to the news items that the learners already have. The learners have to take account of the news items as they produce their newspapers. This idea is reminiscent of what are called 'Newspaper Days' in schools around the world. Pupils are encouraged to produce their own school newspaper using a range of technology skills. These papers are often produced with schools from different countries collaborating and messages are exchanged in a number of languages to suit those that are being taught in the relevant schools. In the UK these activities are often sponsored by local or regional newspapers and the quality of the final product can be very high.

Technology has changed dramatically since the period when Jones, F (ibid.) described his activity and the World Wide Web has made access to 'news' information very fast and up-to-the-minute. This information is also delivered in a range of digital forms: text, pictures, sound, and video, making access to it very quick and easy. We'll discuss these issues in more detail below, but before we do this let's consider one or two other simulation ideas.

There are many different simulations available in other fields, particularly in science and technology, the humanities and in economics and business. If you are involved in ESP/EAP teaching, finding suitable simulation software is not difficult and making a bridge between languages and other subject teaching, particularly in a formal educational environment like a school, college or university is not difficult. Many subject areas make ready use of this kind of software in subject teaching and learners from these disciplines will be used to them. A quick glance through a recent software catalogue reveals a whole range of titles including *Pizza Tycoon* which sounds very much like a more recent version of *Fast Food*, *Arcventure 1 – The Romans* where learners join an archaeological dig, or *Slick*, a program about an oil spillage at sea.

An interesting, but again very simple program that can be used with business English learners is one that is called *Sucker*. This is similar to *Fast Food*, but has the advantage that all of the learners work from the same program, in a sense forcing the teacher and learners to be organised in the work that they do. The main idea is to keep a vacuum cleaner company running and in profit for a twelve-month period. You only have to adjust two variables for each month's trading: the number you want to sell and the price. There are certain fixed costs that you have to take into account and there are a number of random elements that can affect your business like strikes or delivery failures. When you make your choice about price and number of machines for the month the computer calculates your profits and losses, displays these on the screen and then you can print them out. The software allows up to ten teams to work at the same time, so with three to six in a group you can manage a reasonable class size. Because it is only one piece of software, potentially you only need one computer for the whole group and this computer does not necessarily need to be in the main classroom. Groups do not need to congregate around the computer to make decisions, this can be done away from the machine. In classes at Manchester learners did other tasks like memo, letter and report writing, and designing a marketing strategy to shift more vacuum cleaners. They also sent only one person to the computer to type in their decisions about price and number for the month. This person then reported the results. The class lasted about two hours and at the end decisions were saved for a further class, thus making time management more effective. A considerable range of language work can then come from one simple program. This is very similar to the newspaper activities described earlier.

Generic software

Even if people do not have access to this kind of specialist material, or do not have regular access to the Web for use with their learners, it is still possible to make use of generic tools for all sorts of interesting activities. Generic tools include packages like word processors, spreadsheets and databases and are widely available in business and educational contexts and increasingly in the home. This kind of software can be used in a number of different ways for promoting different language skills including speaking. The activities can easily be adapted to business, ESP, or young learner groups and can be undertaken in computer rooms, in self-access centres, or at home. A simple activity using databases or spreadsheets is to collect information about learners in the group via questionnaires. This information is then entered into the database (many spreadsheets have similar functions these days) and then the data is investigated to learn things about the students, e.g. how many of them have brothers and sisters, what hobbies they have in common, how many of them smoke or enjoy eating out and so on. Software like this has the capability of producing a variety of charts and graphs which can be used to talk or write about.

Databases

A typical lesson with databases might be as follows:

Equipment required: at least one computer with suitable database software.

1. If you have not used them before, ask the group what they think a questionnaire is and why people use them. You can perhaps show examples of different kinds of questionnaires. You could also start the class by introducing the concept of a database, getting the students to do some investigations on an already made up dataset if you have the computers available.

2. Either introduce a topic, or get the learners to decide on a suitable topic for a questionnaire. Examples might be about the family, study habits, clothes, music, films etc.

3. In small groups get the learners to think of questions they might put on a questionnaire. The aim of this is to have some practice in writing question forms and for the teacher to see if any remedial work is necessary.

4. Select ten questions to put on the questionnaire. This can be done by various means according to the group and teacher preferences. Depending on the aim of the activity the questions can either be typed up by the groups, by (a) volunteer(s), or by the teacher.

5. The next phase is to try out the questionnaire on the group and collect in the data. How you deal with the data is then a matter of choice, depending on whether you want to teach the learners how to use a database, or whether again the teacher or willing volunteer(s) enters the data in themselves. At this point you can look at the data either using the database search facilities, or via graphs and charts. The questionnaire can then be altered if necessary and if wished tried out on larger groups, other classes in a school, friends, parents and so on. This subsequent data can be added in and again used to investigate various issues.

6. Data-handling is a very common feature of many lessons in schools and forms the backbone of much research. Once the learners have mastered the basic ideas of what data is, how it can be collected and represented, they can then go on to look at larger datasets and do more sophisticated analysis either for presentations or for reports.

This kind of real-life task can be highly motivating and does not need a lot of technology or sophisticated software to be effective. Databases are used widely in society and in many educational contexts. The ideas described above can also be used as the basis of wider project work. Materials from the survey can be written up and included in a class/ school newspaper (see above). These activities require a lot of spoken language work, much of which is away from the computer.

Spreadsheets

Similar work can be done with spreadsheets. Two interesting lessons which involve spreadsheets are described by Copland (1995: 10–12). He is not interested in teaching his learners how to enter data into spreadsheets, but uses already set up material to run business simulations. In his opening remarks he talks about the fact that *Fast Food* is after all a kind of spreadsheet program. His first example is based on a textbook activity from *Cambridge English 2* and is about personal budgeting. Learners working in groups have to reduce their monthly spending by 20% so that they can pay off a bank overdraft. When they have made their choices, they print out a graph based on their calculations and write about how they came to their decisions. In some ways this is similar to the earlier simulation that describes energy consumption in the home.

The second activity is more business oriented, but takes into account the increasing need for people to interpret graphs and charts as part of their daily, business, or academic life. These visuals also form an increasing part of ELT examinations e.g. IELTS, or CCSE. Students were given the task of increasing expenditure in a number of departments within a company and then writing up a report on their activity for the company newsletter. Learners worked in groups around the computers and talked about the task in hand.

As Copland points out, although many teachers may not want to learn spreadsheets, in many institutions these packages already sit on the network and a number of simulation activities can be built up quite quickly and used for a range of classes.

This section has looked at a range of commercial products and the research that has gone into their use for promoting spoken language using computers. It has also pointed out that there are a number of different ways that computers can be used as part of project or group work to help motivate learners, or to drive forward an activity.

Using computers to communicate

Most people would agree that computers have revolutionised the way people communicate. The jury is still out as to whether computer-mediated communication (CMC) can enhance spoken language, although research is giving us strong indications that this may be the case (see below). This type of activity has featured widely in the literature since the early 90s and seems to be taking hold as one of the preferred ways of making use of computers for language teaching.

The developments of CMC have been accelerated by the development of the Internet. The growth of the World Wide Web has been exponential and has captured the imagination of many teachers who are exploiting the ability of the Internet to bring the outside world into the classroom and to enable learners to communicate with other learners all over the world.

Think for a few minutes about what areas of Internet communications you are aware of. You may of heard of IRC, MUDs and MOOs, listservs, graffiti walls and the like, but may not be entirely sure what they all are and how they can be used in ELT.

Let's start off with some definitions.

One of the main reasons that communications have become so central is that they will work with any system. You are not constrained by what computer you have. If we have state of the art PCs and you have a Mac Classic or use UNIX, we can still talk to each other. The same is true of the WWW where any machine can access the basic information that is presented there, although you do need something more advanced for sound and moving images.

The most basic form of communication on any network is e-mail (electronic mail).

We have used the term network rather than Internet here to remind people that activities can be conducted without reference to the Internet at all. It may be that a school has a small internal network and that people can communicate on the system inside the organisation. Many large companies work like this, they only allow their employees access to an internal system. This is often these days referred to as an *intranet*.

E-mail allows a range of messages to be sent, read and responded to at different times. A message can be sent, read and replied to very quickly, or there can be a delay of several days before a message is answered. This makes e-mail more versatile than other forms of 'written' communication. Faxes can be quick, but not that quick, whereas e-mail can actually be part of an ongoing lesson if the systems are working fast enough and the relevant groups are in the right place at the right time. The second form of communication, often called *asynchronous* communication, is the more common use of e-mail. This is where messages are sent, but are then picked up at a later time and are replied to after the content has been considered. There is therefore a delay in messages moving about the system.

Another general feature of simple e-mail is that it is often one-to-one communication like letters. See the appendix to Burbidge et al (1996) for the relationship between e-mail and letter writing. However, it can be one to many and it is very easy to send copies of an e-mail message to other people. So a teacher can be kept involved in ongoing 'conversations' between groups of students.

At the next level we can make use of listservs, bulletin boards, graffiti walls and computer conferencing software. These are ways of distributing messages more widely on a network. A listserv is a way of automatically sending messages to a group of people with like interests. They can be small groups with specific interests, or very large ones like TESL-L which also has a number of subgroups. TESL-L is a large e-mail distribution list run out of City University New York by Anthea Tillyer. E-mail distribution lists enable you to send a message to one common e-mail address and these are then re-sent automatically to everyone who is a member of that list. In order to be part of a group you need to subscribe. This means sending a message to a particular e-mail address and a semi-automated piece of software will add you to the list and then start sending you messages from other members of the list as it receives them. A bulletin board or graffiti wall are similar, but with these you post your message on to a particular site either by adding a message or by filling in a form on the WWW. Your message then appears on this 'board', or 'wall' for everyone to see. The advantage of this is that you do not get lots of messages in your e-mail every day and that you do not have to be a member of a particular group. You can read without subscribing. Listservs, bulletin boards and graffiti walls are all asynchronous. Computer conferencing software can play the role of a number of different systems, it can be used for e-mail, bulletin boards and chat (see below) in one combined area. Commonly discussed systems include *First Class*, used a great deal by the Open University in the UK and mentioned in Scrimshaw (1993), or *Lotus Notes* which is a very interesting environment for computer-based learning. See Jones and O'Brien (1997). These environments have some advantages over other facilities, but of course they assume that everyone has the software, which can be expensive for an institution running such courses. *Lotus Notes* as illustrated in the Jones and O'Brien article and *First Class* are probably best used in an organisational environment where everyone is using the system and there is sufficient technical backup. There are also freely available sites on the Web that provide similar functionality and where the technical side is managed by someone else. These environments have often been created as parts of research projects, or are provided by an educational charity.

Another group of facilities on the Internet are synchronous forms of communication. E-mail can be, but it is generally accepted that IRC – Internet Relay Chat, MUDs – Multiple User Domains and MOOs – MUD Object Oriented Domains can be used for real time communication. See a range of articles by Lesley Shield et al. at http://halley.yadata. com.br/schMOOze/Publications/. The aim of these facilities is for two or more people to meet together and have a 'conversation' using text. There are a number of special sites designed specifically for ELT learners and their teachers, the most famous probably being SchMOOze University (http://schmooze.hunter.cuny.edu:8888/), but it is possible to find a large range of chat sites and MOOs to suit all interests (and I mean all!). Many commercial Internet providers like *Compuserve* and *AOL* also have their own internal chat systems which are open to subscribers only, but offer similar functionality.

With the rapid growth of the WWW and the increase in speed of access to the Internet, other forms of Internet communication become increasingly feasible. These make use of such tools as *CU-SeeMe* and real-time audio built into browsers like *Communicator*. *CU-SeeMe* is an Internet videoconferencing facility. Other forms of audio- and video-conferencing have been used in the ELT field, but these can be very expensive and only institutions with considerable facilities can hope to make use of these more powerful systems. See Jennings (1995) for a discussion of one such European project. Video-conferencing is much more common in professions like medicine and is beginning to replace face-to-face meetings in business.

You are probably aware that there is some debate about the kind of discourse that computer conferencing is. In the discussion above I have put 'written' and 'conversation' into inverted commas. This has been done to raise awareness of this issue.

Think about your e-mail communications and the kind of language that you make use of. Are they written language, or spoken language written down: what Daiute (1985: 291) describes as 'talky writing'?

Recent literature has abounded with discussions of the use of e-mail particularly in ELT, but as Robinson (1993: 111) points out, e-mail in education is a 'relatively recent phenomenon'. In other areas of language teaching (modern languages in the UK) there seems to have been more interest earlier on. Brown (1988) reports early experiments in the learning of French using e-mail. A more recent example for the teaching of German is St John and Cash (1995). The first significant article in a regular ELT journal was Soh and Soon (1991) who describe a cultural interaction project. Pennington and Stevens (1992) hardly mention e-mail, but there then follows a significant increase in articles in the area, culminating in two books by Warschauer (1995a, 1995b), a chapter in Pennington (1996), a book on the Internet and language teaching from Sperling (1997) and a whole raft of reports and articles in the last two years both in print, in listserv archives and on the Web. Recent international conferences have also concentrated on this area.

Clearly this must be a very important area considering the amount published and both teachers and learners find this something that is motivating. Why is this?

You might like to spend a few minutes reflecting on why the communications revolution appears to be having such an impact on ELT more recently and whether you think that it will remain an important area and why.

Most of the use of communications technologies in ELT so far have been with e-mail. But uses on the WWW are catching up (see below). Warschauer (1995a: 8) compares e-mail to other more traditional forms of communication to suggest why e-mail is so popular:

E-MAIL VERSUS MAIL, FAX AND TELEPHONE				
Characteristic	E-mail	Mail	Fax	Telephone
Transmits at high speed	yes	no	yes	yes
Transmits a large quantity of information	yes	yes	yes	no
Allows easy data management	yes	no	no	no
Allows transmission of one to many	yes	no	no	no
Costs little	yes	?	?	?

Warschauer, 1995a

There are some points in this table that we would dispute, the main one being cost. Warschauer comes from a US university background where costs of e-mail are hidden. This cost factor will also be an even more important consideration in other parts of the world. Eastment (1996b: 14) in a report commissioned and available from the British Council in print or electronic form, points out:

For the 10% of Londoners who are unemployed, a new US$1,500 computer would represent about six months' total income. For the 45% of Indonesians who are 'underemployed', it represents several years' cash income. The cost of a modem in India is four times as much as in the US, even without taking into account the huge differences in the standards of living.

This is actually a very interesting report (now updated, 1999) and should be widely read. It also has some useful appendices.

On the positive side we would also reinforce the point made earlier that if you are communicating on a network you are not constrained by the computers that you have; they will happily talk to each other.

What sort of things do people do with e-mail?

We have already mentioned the exchange of cultural information and project work that featured as part of the Soh and Soon article (1991), but what else can be done?

Another very common use of e-mail is that of keypals. This is an extension of letter writing and is a variation on penpals. It is not too difficult to find other classes who would like to send and receive messages from your students via e-mail. It can, of course, have its difficulties and sometimes people do not respond to your messages in the same way that they do not respond to letters or faxes. See Sutherland and Black (1993),

Warschauer (1995a & b), or Kappus (1996) for recent discussions. The article mentioned in the paragraph above also starts from this premise.

An interesting project that is mentioned by Warschauer (1995a: 98–99), but which you can read about on the WWW and join in with (we tried it briefly with our group of trainee teachers) is a project run at the Helsinki University of Technology (HUT) by Ruth Vilmi. This is an interesting project because it tries to do a number of things with Internet resources and shows some of the strengths and weaknesses of such an enterprise. As it is based at a university of technology it is quite ESP-based, but this is not to say that general language groups are not welcomed.

The basic project is linked around e-mail and producing text for publication on the WWW, but there are also now some game elements built in.

The project started in 1993 with around 80 students and eight universities involved. Vilmi continues (updating)

> The students themselves represented about twenty nationalities. Each group, or triad (ideally six students, two from each university), exchanged many letters on a certain topic of their choice. They also did research in the library and used the Internet information sources. This culminated in an oral presentation and an academic paper, in most cases a research paper. Many classes exchanged photos, maps and pictures of their country of residence and some classes also exchanged scanned photos via the Internet.

To give you an example of messages that were exchanged, here are some of the contributions from our own and other students. There are three examples illustrating different aspects of project development. They are presented here as I received them.

First, an introduction:

To: email-project@hut.fi
Subject: man-introduction

Born in a small town in the state of Perak in Malaysia about thirty six years ago,I received my early education in a Convent school. After my secondary education, I entered the Teachers' trainning college for two years. My first posting was in Perlis which is the northern most state of Malaysia. I was there for two years after which I got a transfer back to my home town – Sitiawan, Perak, Malayisa.I didn't stay long in the new school either because, after getting married, I followed my husband to Selangor the following year. I got a school nearby my resident and I was teaching English all the time apart from other subjects.I did my diploma in ESL in 1988/89 and here I am in Manchester doing my degree course in TESOL. Hopefully, I'll be doing well in this course so that when I return to Malaysia in July 1996, I'll be a better English teacher to the students who need all the help there is. Besides teaching, I love to cook (only to my family), tidy the house, reading and travelling of course.If there's time, my family and I love to do some shopping together. As far as possible I prefer to do things with my family around. Although the children (a boy aged 10 and a girl aged 6) are naughty at times but it can be fun having them around you most of the time.

Then something a bit lighter:

To: email-project@hut.fi
Subject: EU-joke

Gooooooood morning everybody.

Today is booring and rainy day here in Helsinki. Because that I tell you some joke, about people in the EU. Enjoy ...

A frenchman, an Englishamn, a Swede, A Norwegian and a Finn were in a airpalne which was flying from London to New York.

They were half way across the Atlantic when the plane suddenly started to lose height. The pilot shouted, 'Throw out all your luggage !!'

For a while this helped but soon the plane started to lose height again. The pilot shouted, 'Someone have to jump out to help save the others'. So the Englishman jumped out shouting 'Long live te Queen!' But soon the palne was losing height again. So the Frenchman jumped out shouting 'Long live the Liberty!'.

The plane was nearly in New York when the pilot informed again that somebody must to jump out. Then the Norwegian and Finn saw each others, caught hold of the Swede and threw him out shouting 'Long live Nordiv co-operation!'

Have a nice day !!

Finally, something more academic with a business English flavour:

To: email-project@hut.fi
Subject: Currency problems in the EU

The European Union would be a great advance as far as globalization is concerned...but the EU members are far from developing the single currency. single currency means that soem countries would lose something they covert, economic sovreignty. The Brits and the Germans, the most economically mature countries, would never lump their currency into one with the likes of the Portuguese Escudo and the Italian Lira. I think this is a major obstacle and a philosophical difference that won't be solved for some time.

I think that the idea od Russian involvement in the EU is pretty far off in the future also. The Russians are having a difficult time worrying about internal problems like organized crime so they aren't too concerned about getting involved in the Union. Once they clean their territories up, however they would be invaluable assets to the EU.

Just a few thoughts.

The messages speak for themselves. They reflect a number of different styles and genres. They also reflect considerable extra effort beyond the classroom for most of the students. Although Vilmi in her article reports a number of difficulties, the project still continues and has developed considerably since these original ideas.

For an overview of other activities for use by language teachers, both of Warschauer's books give you a good insight into what can be done. If you find it difficult to get hold of these books, you can get much of the same information by having a look in the TESL-L archives listserv@cunyvm.cuny.edu

In order to access the archives you need to subscribe to the list. Joining and leaving the lists is very simple, you send the message below to the following e-mail address – *listserv@cunyvm.cuny.edu.*

You leave the subject line blank and then in the body of the message type:

sub TESL-L firstname lastname

e.g. *sub TESL-L Paul Brett*

This is all you have to do. Remember it is as well to turn off your signature file as the automated system that joins you to the list cannot cope with other extra bits of information.

The first message you get back will tell you that you have been joined to the list successfully and will send you a file that gives you information about how the list works. It is best if you print this out and read it carefully so that you can understand how to manage your messages more effectively.

If you find the flow of messages too much you can tell the system to send you a daily digest. In order to do this you send another message to *listserv@cunyvm.cuny.edu* saying:

set TESL-L index

You can, of course, unsubscribe from the system as well:

unsubscribe TESL-L Firstname Lastname

Other commands for managing the system come with the introductory material.

As well as reading messages, you can send them in too. In order to send a message you use a different address:

TESL-L@cunyvm.cuny.edu

This time you can add both a subject and a signature file.

If you are interested in general EFL/ESL issues, then subscription to the main list is recommended; however, this does generate a lot of e-mail each day. If you are more interested in computers in language learning, I would recommend TESLCA-L which is about the area of computer-assisted language learning. This is a sub-list of the main one and you have to be a member of the main list to subscribe to the sub-lists, but the subscription procedure is the same. You can be a member of a sub-list without receiving the main postings of TESL-L. This is achieved by sending the following command to the listserv:

set TESL-L nomail

Accessing the TESL-L archives, or the archives of other lists is also an easy option. These archives contain all the postings in the last few years including bibliographies and example lessons organised into topic groups. To access these files, first send a message to the listserv as follows:

index TESL-L

This will send you a list of the files available. When you have made your selection you then send another message as follows:

get xxx xxx TESL-L F=mail

e.g. *get email projects TESL-L F=mail*

There are a large number of other lists relevant to language teachers including the LINGUIST List and SLART-L (Second language acquisition research and teaching) which you can join if you wish. These also have archive facilities. Finding suitable resources and references for working with your learners is a few key strokes away.

There are of course people who feel less buoyant about the role of computer networks in teacher/language teaching and Robinson has a nice table which summarises the positive and negative aspects (1993: 121):

FEATURES OF COMMUNICATION THROUGH COMPUTERS		
	Potential advantages	**Potential disadvantages**
Lack of face-to-face clues	• anonymity • reduction in status	• reduced feedback • impersonal clues • jokes and feelings difficult to convey
	• task-focused (less interpersonal distraction) • reduced pressure on individuals to contribute • increased importance of logical argument • contributions not restricted by turn-taking • less domination by an individual	• more attenuated interaction • reduced pressure on individuals to contribute • need for skilled moderator to control, orchestrate (or censor?) • increased emotion or aggression in messages ('flaming')
Time-lag between responses	• opportunity to reflect before responding • opportunity to reformulate and correct messages before sending • convenience • access to discussion with others	• loss of impetus to reply • slowness in decision-making • reduction of language exchanges for social purposes only • difficulty of reaching consensus

As with many of these lists, positive and negative aspects can seem to cancel each other out, but for some groups, particularly groups that are at a distance anyway, the advantages of having increased communication are likely to outweigh the disadvantages.

The World Wide Web and communications

A number of mentions have been made of the Web in relation both to games and simulations and to enhancing communication activities. So, we will finish off this chapter with a couple of examples of what can be achieved with this relatively new and exciting medium. It will also provide pointers to a range of sites that you can visit to see the various ways that the Web is being used to aid language learners.

Let's go back to the idea of simulations that we were discussing earlier. We talked both about news activities and business simulations. The Web has a whole range of news material available in a variety of formats. It has daily newspapers, radio news, video clips and information from magazines to name a few.

Teachers and learners can make use of this news media in all sorts of ways (see Brett's chapter in this book). Text and pictures can simply be downloaded and made into worksheets. The Web can be searched for information on specific topics by the learners who make use of this material as part of presentations. Using the Web in class live can be frustrating if your link to it is slow, or you find that the site that you had identified is not accessible. Software now exists to enable you to download (the technical term is *cache*) Web pages on to a local fileserver where they can be stored for future use. One program that can be used for this is called *Web Whacker* which is downloadable off the Web. The most recent version of *Internet Explorer* (currently 5), allows you to do the same.

Learners can be working in groups on a specific news area. Individual members of the team can be sent off to the computer to access the Web to find specific information, or late breaking stories. This would have a similar effect to the ideas discussed in the Jones, F (1991) article mentioned earlier. Learners then use the information they have gathered in various ways. If you have the technology available to your students, then the nature of the newspaper need not necessarily be print, it could be a multimedia product.

Along with news media, business material exists on the Web in large quantities. Sibbons (1997) reviews very briefly two activities, one with newspapers again and one on business report writing. If you would like to have a look at what is a very brief report here is the address: http://www.paddocks64.Freeserve.co.uk/CompSIG2/15march.htm

Two starting points for investigations of the Web would be Eastment (1996a & b) and Carrier (1997). Eastment's (1996b) article covers some of the background material that has been discussed here, but has a useful starter list of sites. Carrier's piece in *ELTJ* is a survey review of Web sites for language teaching. If you cannot access this have a look at the Useful Links section of the IATEFL pages. This is not a comprehensive list, but will get you started if you're not already looking.

Bibilography

Brown E (1988) *Learning Languages with Technology* NCET

Burbidge N et al. (1996) *Letters* Oxford University Press

Carrier M (1997) ELT online: the rise of the Internet *ELT Journal 51/3*

Copland C (1995) A piece of the pie *CALL Review*

Dauite C (1985) *Writing and Computers* Addison Wesley

Eastment D (1996a) The Internet for teachers and learners *MET 5/2*

Eastment D (1996b) *The Internet and ELT: the impact of the Internet on ELT* The British Council

Eastment D (1999) *The Internet and ELT: the impact of the Internet on ELT* Summertown Publishing

Harrison C & A Cheung (1992) Microcomputer adventure games in second language acquisition: a study of Hong Kong tertiary students. In Pennington M & V Stevens (1992)

Jennings C (1995) Virtual language schools: overcoming the problem of distance in the training of language teachers. In Howard R & I McGrath (1995) *Distance Education for Language Teachers* Multilingual Matters.

Jones C & T O'Brien (1997) The long and bumpy road to multi-media: hi-tech experiments in teaching a professional genre at a distance *System 25/2*

Jones C & S Fortescue (1987/1991) *Computers in the Language Classroom* Longman

Jones F (1991) Mickey-mouse and state-of-the art: program sophistication and classroom methodology in communicative CALL *System Vol 19 1/2*

Jones G (1986) Computer simulations in language teaching – the Kingdom experiment *System 14/2*

Jones K (1982) *Simulations in Language Teaching* Cambridge University Press

Kappus E (1996) Electronic encounters *TESOL Journal* Winter

Legenhausen L & D Wolff (1988) Computer simulation in language learning: observing *Granville* in the foreign language classroom. In Jung U O H (Ed.) *Computers in Applied Linguistics and Language Learning: The CALL Handbook* Peter Lang

McFarlane A (1997) *Information Technology and Authentic Learning* Routledge

Pennington M (Ed.) (1989) *Teaching Languages with Computers: The State of the Art* Athelstan

Pennington M (Ed.) (1996) *The Power of CALL* Athelstan

Phillips M (1987) *Communicative Language Teaching and the Microcomputer* The British Council

Robinson B (1993) Communicating through computers in the classroom. In Scrimshaw P (Ed.) (1993) *Language, classrooms & computers* Routledge

Scrimshaw P (Ed.) (1993) *Language, classrooms and computers* Routledge

Sibbons A (1997) Review of using the WWW as a business English resource http://www.man.ac.uk/IATEFL/callsig/callsig.htm

Soh B-L & Y-P Soon (1991) English by Email: Creating a Global Classroom via the Medium of Computer Technology *ELTJ 45/4*

Sperling D (1997) *The Internet Guide for English Language Teachers* Prentice Hall

St John E & D Cash (1995) German language learning via email: a case study *ReCALL 7/2*

Sutherland J & P Black (1993) Finding Common Ground: International Email Penpals *CAELL Journal 4/2*

Straker A (1989) *Children using computers* Blackwell

Straker A & H Govier (1997) *Children using computers* Blackwell

Vilmi R (Updating) Global communication through email: http://www.hut.fi/~rvilmi/Project/

Warschauer M (1995a) *Email for English Teaching* TESOL Inc

Warschauer M (Ed.) (1995b) *Virtual connections: online activities and projects for networking language learners* Manoa, University of Hawaii: Second Language Teaching and Curriculum Center

Warschauer M, L Turbee & B Roberts (1996) Computer learning networks and student empowerment *System* 24/1

World Wide Web addresses

What follows is a list of Web addresses referred to in the text and one or two more to get you started if you are not used to using the Web.

Computer Mediated Communication	http://www.december.com/cmc/info
CUSeeMe	http://www.cuseemeworld.com/
IATEFL Pages for CALL SIG, BESIG & Useful Links	http://www.iatefl.org/
Dave Sperling's ESL Café	http://www.eslcafe.com/
Ruth Vilmi's Web project	http://www.hut.fi/~rvilmi/Project/
Web Whacker	http://www.bluesquirrel.com/products/whacker/whacker.html

For other useful links have a look at my own Centre's website:
http://www.man.ac.uk/CELSE

6 Computers in language testing

Glenn Fulcher, *University of Surrey*

Glenn Fulcher has worked in TESOL as a teacher and teacher trainer overseas and in the United Kingdom since 1982. He gained his MA in Applied Linguistics from the University of Birmingham in 1987, and his PhD from the University of Lancaster in 1993. He has a special interest in Language Testing, and is currently on the TOEFL Committee of Examiners. He has also served on the Executive Board of the International Language Testing Association. He is currently Director of the English Language Institute at the University of Surrey, where he teaches language testing and Applied Linguistics on the MA in TESOL and MSc in English Language Teaching.   g.fulcher@surrey.ac.uk

Introduction

Computers have played a key role in language testing since 1935. From the early scoring devices to the latest Computer Adaptive Tests (CATs), computers have come to play a major role in test construction, item banking, test administration, scoring, data analysis, report generating, research, and the dissemination of research. As the machines and software have become more sophisticated, a range of practical, research and ethical issues have arisen. This chapter will outline the role of the computer in language testing and discuss some of the complex issues that need to be addressed in the first decades of the 21st century.

The IBM model 805

The first recorded use of a 'computer' in language testing dates back to 1935 when the IBM model 805 became commercially available. It was the first machine capable of scoring objective tests, and was immediately put into use in the United States to reduce the labour intensive and costly business of scoring millions of tests taken each year. The machine was developed specifically to score multiple choice items that were used in the 'new-type tests' of the day. The new-type test design had been imported from educational testing into language testing during the First World War, for the construction of the army Alpha tests. In the 1920s new-type tests were taken up in school assessment in order to cope with the rapid expansion of schooling provision across the United States. They could be produced and administered efficiently on the industrial scale that was now required (see Spolsky, 1995: 33–51), and automatic marking made possible by the IBM 805 ensured that the multiple choice item would remain the bedrock of educational testing until the present day.

The practical need to assess large numbers of people cheaply and efficiently, and the advent of the technology to achieve this, sat happily alongside the theoretical concerns of testing and assessment specialists. It had long been known that there was error associated with test scores (Edgeworth, 1888; 1890), and the foundations of educational testing and assessment were built upon the concept of reliability, developed at the beginning of the century by researchers like Thorndike (1904) and Spearman (1907; 1913). The statistical tools were supplemented in the 1920s with the development of methods to analyse the properties of test items. There was confidence that the new-type tests provided a practical solution to problems in educational assessment, especially the theoretical (and ethical) problems of reliability. Wood (1927) was among the first to undertake the task of reducing the element of chance in taking tests in large-scale language assessment. He was especially concerned with producing tests that would help place students in homogenous classes in New York schools to avoid the learning and teaching problems that existed at the time. Or, as he put it, to avoid having unhappy students in classes where making progress in language learning was a matter of pure chance.

There was a great deal of debate concerning the value of the new-type tests and the limitations of what can be tested using multiple choice items throughout the 1920s and 1930s (Barnwell, 1996: 49). The debate still continues, although those who weigh up the pros and cons of objective item types are all too frequently unaware of the fact that today's arguments merely rehearse those conducted 80 years ago. What is important to recognise now is that multiple choice items (and tests constructed of objective items) are not inherently more reliable than other item or task types. Lado's (1961) important distinction between reliability and 'scorability' is very important: it is possible to have poorly constructed, unreliable, but easily scored multiple choice items, and well constructed, reliable, but time consuming speaking tests. The reason why multiple choice items have been used so much for a century is not some innate reliability of the item type, but the simple fact that it can be scored so easily by a machine.

As we will see later, the scorability of tests by machines is still an area of concern and active research in the current generation of computer-based tests (CBTs). This is true for constructed responses as well as responses to objective items, for the same reasons of cost and efficiency (Burstein, 1997).

From scoring to testing

Since the first book on computerised language testing was published (Holtzman, 1970) the literature on computer-based testing has grown exponentially. Not surprisingly, one major theme has been the rapid change in computer technology that has allowed us to move away from simply scoring tests to developing comprehensive language testing software packages. From a scoring machine in 1935 to the powerful, cheap desktop machines we have today, language testers have been continuously trying to put the available technology to use. Bunderson, Inouye and Olsen, (1989: 367–368) wrote:

> The computer revolution has been marked by the growth in power and sophistication of computing resources. The computing power of yesterday's mainframes is routinely surpassed by today's supermicros. Yesterday's ENIAC computer, which filled an entire room, was less powerful than the current generation of microcomputers, which fit on a desktop

It is only when placing this next to another quotation from the same paper (Bunderson et al. 1989: 371) that we realise how fast technology is in fact changing:

The memory capacity of most modern delivery systems is evolving rapidly. Most microcomputer workstations now have half to two megabytes of random access memory. Future workstations will use even larger amounts of random access memory. The early, expensive, mass-storage devices are being replaced by inexpensive, high-density, magnetic and opto-electronic devices. Hard-disk storage exceeding 100 megabytes per workstation is becoming more common.

Any discussion of hardware, memory size, and processing capacity will inevitably be out of date within a few years, if not months, of being written. We must simply assume that the constant development, availability and use of larger and faster computers will be the norm for the foreseeable future.

What are the uses to which language testers have put this technology? In a recent review of the role of computers in language testing, Burstein, Frase, Ginther and Grant (1996), isolated eight areas in which computers are now used in language testing. These may be summarised as:

– Test design: the exchange of written and graphic materials between test designers who may be working in different locations.
– Test construction: including item trials, the main function of the computer is envisaged to be the exchange of written and graphic materials, as well as items, between those involved in item writing and revision.
– Item tryout: Items are delivered in their near-final format, responses are stored on the computer, and item level statistics calculated and stored in a database (itembank) with the test items.
– Test item delivery: the delivery of actual tests from databases, including the collection and storage of responses. Appropriate technologies for test-taker identification should also be considered in this phase of the process.
– Item management: storing and updating item information.
– Item scoring and transforming item responses into test scores.
– Item analysis and interpretation: relating the score to some general interpretative scheme for the score.
– Score reporting: delivering scores and related information.

The authors lamented the fact that the use of computers in language testing had not resulted in the creative use of multimedia elements in the way that has happened in instructional programs. And at the time of writing this paper, there is still little in the way of innovative computer-based tests that contain a creative mix of media. This is because, as Frase (1997: 519) points out: 'the obstacles to the successful use of technology for language testing now seem less technical than conceptual.' We turn briefly to some of these conceptual issues, before considering approaches to computer-based testing.

Concepts, constructs and equity

The computer is ideally suited to the delivery of objective items, particularly multiple choice items. As we have shown, when the first computers that could deliver tests became available, existing language testing theory was compatible with the new technology. Classical Test Theory (CTT) and the statistical tools associated with it were developed to heighten the reliability of objective tests. The first computer-based tests were simply paper and pencil tests that had been designed, constructed and piloted using the tools of CTT. These tests were delivered through the new electronic medium for ease of test administration, delivery and scoring (Alderson, 1988), thus reducing costs even further than had been possible with scoring machines. Recent complex computer adaptive tests (see below for a definition and discussion of CATs) are based on Item Response Theory (IRT) but IRT (and its associated statistical tools) was also developed for the analysis of objective tests.[1] It is therefore not surprising that objective items and contexts that look and feel as if they have been derived from pencil and paper tests continue to appear in computer-based language tests. However, there are other more important reasons why language test designers have been slow to take advantage of the multimedia capability of the computer.

The concerns that language testers have with computer-based tests are not dissimilar from those they have with paper and pencil tests. The most important of these is knowing what the test measures, of the underlying test construct. The ability to make valid inferences from test scores depends upon providing rationales and empirical evidence to support construct validity (Messick, 1989). The introduction of multimedia to a listening test may change the nature of the construct being measured. It is possible that video content changes the process of comprehending listening texts in ways that we do not yet fully understand. Extensive research has not been conducted to discover if the meaning of a score may change because of the visual clues of the medium (Ginther and Chawla, 1997), or whether changes in score meaning are related to test construct or error. Until this research has been done it seems unlikely that test providers such as Educational Testing Services (ETS) will introduce multimedia into the computer-based TOEFL. Construct validity, as an all-inclusive concept, is central to all language testing research. The focus on technology in computer-based and computer adaptive testing is now giving way to the requirements that construct validity be investigated on an on-going basis, as can be seen from the range of papers in a recently published volume on the computer adaptive testing of reading (Chalhoub-Deville, 1999; see also Fulcher, in press for the significance of this volume).

A further major concern is the ethical aspect of computer-based testing. A computer-based test (which is designed to measure the same construct as a paper and pencil based test) should rank order test-takers in approximately the same way as a pencil and paper form of the test, and the two forms should have similar means and standard deviations (APA, 1986). Together these requirements constitute the principle of equivalent forms. Fulcher (1999) reviewed evidence regarding the equivalence of forms, but also considered it important to investigate whether other factors impacted on test scores, such as the test-taker's previous experience with a range of computer uses, their attitudes to technology and taking tests on computers, and whether factors such as age, gender, educational background or L1 would be likely to affect the score on a computer-based test. The issue of the impact of familiarity with computers was also of major concern to ETS prior to the introduction of the computer-based TOEFL in 1998. Kirsch et al. (1998), Eignor et al. (1998), Taylor et al. (1998) and Taylor et al. (1999) investigated the impact of the new delivery medium and found that 16% of test-takers were affected. The solution was to introduce a compulsory tutorial that all test-takers must take immediately before they do the TOEFL CBT. ETS has taken other steps to familiarise potential test-takers with the format and medium, such as the sampler CD, which is available free of charge. In the writing component of the new TOEFL, there is also the option to type the response or answer in long hand, an option designed to 'bias for the best' by letting test-takers select the medium in which they think they will perform better.

The latest edition of the Standards for Educational and Psychological Testing (1999) raises concerns with regard to computer-based tests, which researchers must address in the future. The following standards are particularly relevant to computer-based tests.

– Standard 2.8: In computer-based tests there is a worry that if the test is speeded, there may be a large impact upon the test score, especially if the test is adaptive and the test-taker responds randomly to items towards the end of the test.
– Standard 5.5: Test-takers should be given an opportunity to respond to sample test items (and their responses monitored) unless they are familiar with the equipment and response type already.
– Standard 6.11: If a test can be taken on computer and in paper and pencil format the interchangeability of the scores should be investigated and reported.
– Standard 4.10 and 8.3: Where a test-taker is offered an alternative test form (such as paper and pencil or computer-based form), there should be enough information available about the characteristics of the two forms to allow the test-taker to make an informed decision.

With specific reference to computer adaptive tests:

– Standard 3.12: Technical manuals for CATs should provide information on the procedures for selecting items, the criteria for selecting the starting point and termination point of a test, for scoring, and for controlling for item exposure.
– Standard 13.18: 'Documentation of design, models, scoring algorithms, and methods for scoring and classifying should be provided for tests administered and scored using multimedia or computers. Construct-irrelevant variance pertinent to computer-based testing and the use of other media in testing, such as the test-taker's familiarity with technology and the test format, should be addressed in their design and use.'

It is clear that the further development of computer adaptive tests is not simply a matter of exploiting the power of the computer as quickly as possible, but of constructing a systematic research agenda that investigates the issues involved. It may be for this reason that, while graphics have been introduced into the TOEFL CBT (ETS, 1998), the TOEFL test specifications stop short of using the full multimedia potential of the computer.

Computer adaptive testing

Although any test that is currently delivered using paper and pencil can also be delivered by computer, the most important development of the last decade has been computer adaptive testing, in which the computer branches to certain sub-tests (branching routines) or selects the next test item (adaptive routines) depending upon the response pattern of the individual test-taker. The first CATs were developed in the 1970s (Gruba and Corbel, 1998; Dunkel, 1999: 80) although it is not until recently that they have come into widespread use, generating much research and comment.[2] CATs have been made possible by the extensive use of Item Response Theory, and the development of algorithms that drive the test program to select and deliver test items, score responses, and provide immediate feedback to test-takers. It is beyond the scope of this paper to provide an introduction to IRT methods, but there are a number of excellent texts available for the reader who wishes to learn more about the measurement theory underlying computer adaptive testing.[3]

Bunderson et al. (1989: 381) describe the development of CATs as the second generation of computerised testing, capable of adapting test content on the fly to suit the estimated ability of the test-taker. One of the most advanced CAT systems is *FastTEST*, produced by Assessment Systems Corporation in 1999 as a successor to *MicroCAT*, which was first released in 1984.[4]

Computer adaptive tests constructed and delivered with systems like *FastTEST* have a number of major advantages. Firstly, all items and item level information is contained in an item bank on the local machine or network. Attached to each item is information that is used by the program's algorithm in selecting items or subsets of items for delivery. The information contains item statistics like difficulty, discrimination, and perhaps a guessing parameter. It may also contain information on content, context, or any other tag that would be relevant to item selection for specific purposes testing. This means that test items can be selected to individualise the test by matching it to the test-takers' needs or the requirements of score users. Secondly, the selection of the next item or sub-test is dependent upon the responses of the test-taker. The algorithm may select a more difficult item for learners who get the responses to previous questions correct, and easier items for learners who answer many items incorrectly. Therefore, no test-taker takes exactly the same test as any other, assuming that the item bank is reasonably large. This increases test security. Thirdly, the number of items that the test-taker is required to attempt is reduced, as the computer will terminate the test once an assessment of the test-taker's ability level has been estimated within pre-set error (or other relevant) parameters. Not only does this save time and resources in terms of test delivery and the amount of time needed to administer tests, it also provides instant results and reporting. Taking an adaptive test can therefore be more motivating for many learners. Finally, if a large enough bank of items with very high or low facility values can be constructed, it should in principle be possible to identify students who are extremely able, and those who have very low ability. This is not possible with non-adaptive tests because the test would need to be exceptionally long and contain items with facility values that cover the entire ability range.

However, there are a number of disadvantages associated with CATs. CATs can only work if there is a large number of items in an item bank, which are calibrated to a measurement scale constructed using Item Response Theory. Building up a sufficiently large item bank can be time-consuming and costly. The more parameters the algorithm uses in CAT administration, the larger the sample size needed for pre-testing and calibration. For example, when using a three-parameter model item statistics are unstable using samples of less than 1000 test-takers. If the item bank is not sufficiently large, with sufficient items across the entire ability range of the test-takers, there may be item overexposure (threatening security) or a failure to adequately estimate the ability of very able or very weak students. While the use of calibrated items from a bank allows clearer interpretation of score meaning, achieving this should not be seen as an easy process. Establishing criterion-referenced meaning at various points on a scale, especially for cut scores, requires careful research. This is especially true in CATs where the test-takers are not taking the same test. The third problem associated with the item bank is one of sampling. It is frequently assumed that items are written to adequately reflect the domain to which the score user wishes to make inferences, and the implementation of a CAT means that only a small proportion of the items are selected for any individual test. It is therefore appropriate that the issue of content validity of a CAT is problematised, so that test developers consider whether, and to what degree, the CAT should be forced to include a representative sample of items in the test, even if they are not needed in order to place a student on the ability scale. Finally, in a CAT the test-taker is not allowed to omit items. The reason for this is simply that if learners respond only to items that they think they are going to get right, the ability estimate will be unnaturally high. All items must be answered for the computer to estimate ability reliably, unlike paper and pencil tests where the test-takers have the opportunity to miss items if they wish, and review items if they have time at the end of the test. In CATs, this freedom is removed. As yet, however, there has been no research to suggest that this is demotivating or disadvantageous for any identifiable groups of test-takers.

It can be seen that CATs have major advantages over paper and pencil tests, despite the research that still needs to be conducted before the full potential of the computer can be harnessed in test design. Nevertheless, there is one other issue that requires consideration. In some countries (mainly in the United States) there is legislation requiring the disclosure of test papers (see Brown, 1997: 53). In the United Kingdom, the Department of Education has recently considered introducing legislation to force examination boards to return all examination scripts to students after they have been scored. CATs rely on large secure item banks that are expensive to build and maintain. If the item banks must be periodically disclosed to test-takers, then CATs would become prohibitively expensive. Test developers would be forced back to first generation non-adaptive computer-based tests. While legislators in the United States are aware of these problems and considering disclosure laws in the light of modern test theory and CAT developments, this is not the case in other countries such as the United Kingdom, where there is little awareness of measurement issues.

Despite the growing commercial availability of CAT software with user friendly interfaces that require only a passing knowledge of Windows operating systems to use, teachers and language teaching institutions should beware of moving from conventional testing to computer adaptive testing. Without the resources and expertise to develop and operate the systems, it is better to remain with good conventional tests that produce better quality information within local settings.

Testing on the Internet

Although the Internet, and the World Wide Web in particular, is a global information distribution network that would easily allow the delivery of tests anywhere in the world, its potential has not yet been realised. Nevertheless, the range and variety of Internet-based tests is growing. Links to tests currently available are maintained at the Resources in Language Testing Page, which is frequently updated.[5]

The interactivity that is currently available on the Web is provided by programs stored on the server written in *PERL* script (Practical Extraction and Report Language) or downloaded to the client's machine in *Java*. This allows computer-based tests or CATs to be scored on-line. However, at the time of writing this paper, all on-line tests are available only as low-stakes 'quizzes.' This is mainly because large scale high-stakes test delivery over the Web faces serious security problems. Until the security issues associated with the transfer of information over the Internet have been solved, it is unlikely that testing organisations will use the Web, and will prefer to use third-party computer installations such as those provided by Sylvan.[6] Whilst testing on the web remains non-commercial, it is unlikely that any significant CATs with large item banks will be available within the near future. One exception to this may be DIALANG.[7] Funded by the European Union, the DIALANG project was designed to produce diagnostic tests in 14 European languages delivered as a CAT over the Web (see Alderson, in press). Although not adaptive at item level, the system allows branching routines depending upon an initial self-assessment, and on-going estimation of test-taker ability. When the program is released it is expected to provide feedback to the test-taker on the relationship between self-assessment and estimated ability, and benchmark the estimated ability to Council of Europe proficiency level descriptors.

Until large testing organisations such as ETS are able to utilise the Internet for high-stakes test delivery, first generation computer-based tests will remain a very real option for language testers. The delivery of these traditional CBTs on the Internet is of particular interest, for a variety of reasons.

Firstly, the only software needed to take the tests is a standard browser. These can be loaded onto any type of computer, making the test delivery system truly platform independent. The only requirements relate to hardware (the need for a modem), and a reasonably fast processor to download the information from the host server providing the test. The second important advantage of the Internet as a means of delivery is that the tests can be delivered to any machine linked to the Internet, at any time convenient to the provider and the client. In distance learning programmes such arrangements can be beneficial to both the learner and the tutors.

The Web also provides advantages in the flexibility of test design without the need to resort to third-party plug-ins. It is quite feasible, for example, to use the frames facility of the browser to divide the computer screen into windows, each of which contains a content page. Prompts may be set up on a series of frames that incorporate text, images, audio, and video, where computer links are reliable and quick. In fact, the flexibility of html in designing web pages makes it possible to design a range of novel task types through the imaginative combination of multimedia in a frames environment for low-stakes testing or research (Fulcher, 1998). A further advantage of delivering tests over the Web is that links can be established to information, help facilities, databases, or libraries, to deliver the kind of indirect performance test frequently recommended for placement purposes in academic programmes (see Robinson and Ross, 1996). Tests need no longer be self-contained, watertight units, but involve the use of information from the outside world, to any degree the test designer wishes to incorporate it. This potential can be used to increase the 'authenticity' of some testing activities.

In computer-based testing on the Internet, innovation is possible where there is flexibility over the format and content of the prompt. However, it is not as easy to be as innovative in the area of item type, as we have indicated above. Most Internet browsers support multiple choice, multi-choice, pull-down menu and constructed response item types, and combinations of these. For example, multiple pull-down menus can provide matching or sequencing items. Constructed response items may be of two types: limited constructed response where a word or short phrase is required, and which is automatically scored against a template, and extended constructed response, which must be e-mailed to human raters for scoring. In this respect, little has changed since Alderson (1988) found it difficult to design innovative item types for computer-based language tests.

From a measurement perspective, Internet testing raises many questions that still need to be investigated, as we have argued above. At present, there is not enough research evidence to justify introducing the novelty of what can now be achieved, except for use in low-stakes testing and research. Measurement and ethical questions must be addressed in relation to the Internet, just as they must in developing CAT listening tests with video instead of audio. In summary, we are currently in a situation where innovation and flexibility are possible but implementation is not a pressing concern until the conceptual problems associated with the new medium have been thoroughly researched.

Testing, artificial intelligence and constructed response

The third and fourth generation of computerised testing, as described by Bunderson et al. (1989), whilst visionary, are nevertheless still some way in the future. The third generation of computerised testing is the continuous assessment of learning and the projection of learning trajectories from the current ability level of the student to another ability level at some point in the future. The assumption is that it is possible to calculate trajectories in language learning in a meaningful way. Given what we currently know about language acquisition, including U-shaped and discontinuous learning (Larsen-Freeman and Long, 1991: 105–107; Perkins et al., 1996), and taking into account the multitude of variables that affect language learning, it seems unlikely that the progress of individuals can be meaningfully predicted very far into the future.

This makes it more unlikely that we will see the development of the predicted fourth generation of assessment (Bunderson et al. 1989: 398–402), in which artificial intelligence will be brought to bear on continuous measurement in order to provide advice on learning style and content selection for the learner, related to the current estimated stage of learning. This fourth generation of tests would have all the properties of the third generation, but would be linked to expert second language acquisition systems. The field of second language acquisition is currently not able to provide such an expert system, and even if a model of language development could be generally agreed, calibrating the test to the theoretical model would be a major project that would occupy researchers for many years.

In recent years there have been a number of significant advances. We review two here, both relating to the scorability of constructed responses.

Bernstein (1997) reports on the development of *PhonePass*™, which is a test of speaking conducted over the telephone with a computer.[8] The testing system relies on the computer being able to match the pronunciation of the speaker on any given word using a statistical model derived from a large database of (intelligible) native speakers of American English, and evaluating the rate of delivery. The test takes ten minutes, and diagnostic sub-scores are returned for reciting/pronunciation, reading fluency, repeat accuracy, repeat fluency, and listening vocabulary. Ordinate, the company that has developed *PhonePass*, is unusual among private testing companies (and, for that matter, public examination boards in the UK!) in that it has conducted extensive research into the reliability and validity of the system it has developed. Ordinate reports reliability coefficients for *PhonePass* that are comparable (and sometimes higher) than human raters, and overall correlations between scores awarded by human judges and *PhonePass* of .93. Ordinate has also commissioned a number of studies to investigate its reliability and validity, and made these available on the Internet in portable document format (Bernstein, 1998; 1999a; 1999b).

The problem with a test like *PhonePass* is that it relies for its validity on the correlation with direct measures such as the Oral Proficiency Interview (OPI). It is possible that an estimate of speech rate would correlate with a direct test of speaking, just as it is possible that the height of a learner in Spain would correlate with a measure of vocabulary size. These factors are related through other variables. Yet, it would be difficult to claim that measuring height and making an inference about language ability had any construct validity. The definition of 'fluency' in *PhonePass* (Bernstein, 1998) as rhythm, phrasing and pausing is far from the complex applied linguistic notions that are used in non-computerised test development (Fulcher, 1996). Nevertheless, it is work like that of Bernstein that will lead to continued improvement in speech recognition technology. This may ultimately lead to a new generation of automated speaking tests that could support stronger construct claims. In the meantime, Ordinate can offer a cheap on-demand test that is certainly predictive of speaking ability, even if its construct validity may be questioned.

Another exciting development concerns the e-rater,[9] developed by ETS primarily for use on Graduate Management Admission Test (GMAT) and the Graduate Record Examinations (GRE) to rate essays. Research has also been conducted into the ability of e-rater to automatically score writing from non-native speakers of English using scripts from the Test of Written English (TWE). Burstein and Chodorow (1999) report agreement between e-rater and human graders in 92% of cases. E-rater automatically builds models for individual writing prompts using large numbers of human scored writing samples, based on 52 syntactic, discourse and topic variables. It then matches new writing samples against the model to produce the score. Initial research shows that e-rater performs differentially across language groups, and future research at ETS is likely to concentrate on whether different models are needed for different language groups. It should of course be stressed that e-rater is a research project. It is being used operationally only in conjunction with human raters, and is not being used operationally at all with non-native writers.

In these two examples, we can see the issue of scorability – this time with constructed response tests. While *PhonePass* can be criticised for relying heavily on correlational evidence for its validity, the e-rater represents a contribution to construct research. The advances in natural language processing since the reviews of Freedle (1990) mean that the process of machine rating has started to become much more like the process of human rating in the consideration of linguistic elements of the text. It is fair to say that the e-rater represents the first application of artificial intelligence that may successfully help with construct definition.

Communication and the dissemination of research

It may be noticed that many of the sources cited in this chapter are available on-line. Perhaps one of the enduring benefits of computers to language testing will be the speed and ease of communication, and the availability of information. This is achieved through discussion lists dedicated to language testing issues and web sites devoted to the transmission of language testing and measurement information.

LTEST-L remains the active open discussion list of testing issues. ILTA-MEM is the list of the International Language Testing Association (ILTA), and is only open to members. Together, these lists allow the speedy transmission of information, and keep teachers and researchers in touch with the latest developments in the field.

On the Web, sites such as *Assessment and Evaluation on the Internet* (http://ericae.net/ nintbod.htm) and the *Resources in Language Testing Page* (http://www.surrey.ac.uk/ ELI/ltr.html) provide electronic focal points for the dissemination of information. The latter, now receiving reviews in text publications such as Sperling (1998) and Douglas (2000), provides an electronic hub for language testing in particular. The Home Page of ILTA is maintained at the same site, which has recently been expanded to contain a series of introductory videos on language testing for language teachers (Fulcher and Thrasher, on-line). This novel approach to dissemination of language testing information is part of a strategy to achieve the educational objectives of ILTA. The page is now being used in introductory language testing courses for teachers in South America, Europe and the Far East.

Test-takers also have access to information about the tests they may have to take, and can download sample papers and advice on test-taking. The University of Cambridge Local Examinations Syndicate maintains a download page with handbooks and sample papers for most of its tests (http://www.cambridge-efl.org/support/dloads/index.html). ETS offers the same for TOEFL, but adds information on test-taking for learners with disabilities, tutorials, a download library, order forms for free sample disks, and a store to purchase preparation materials (http://www.toefl.org/).

Researchers, teachers and test-takers therefore have more information on language testing available than ever before, and this would not have been possible without Internet communication.

Conclusions

The use of computers in language testing, and the use of computer adaptive tests, has gone beyond the stage of discussing how technology can lead to innovation in design that was prevalent even a few years ago. Nevertheless, as long as scorability remains an issue in large testing programs where cost is an important factor, we will continue to see researchers trial any solution that automates the process.

The real focus in the coming years will be on conducting research that addresses the fundamental questions that must be asked about any test, any testing procedure or system, whether paper- or computer-based: what inferences can be drawn from the test scores. Some scorability research, like that into the e-rater, will help here, because the researchers are trying to copy in the program what human raters respond to in text and, in the process, help clarify the construct of writing ability. The issue that will dominate discussion and research on computers in language testing in the next decade, as Chalhoub-Deville (1999: x) rightly predicts, will be test construct.

Notes

[1] For a clear explanation of CTT and IRT and their associated statistical tools see Davidson F (in press) 'The Language Tester's Statistical Toolbox'. In Fulcher G (Ed.) Expanding perspectives on language testing in the 21st century. Special Edition of *System 28 4*

[2] For recent technical reviews of the potential advantages and disadvantages of computer adaptive testing see Brown, 1997; Chalhoub-Deville et al, 1997; Chalhoub-Deville & Deville, 1999; Dunkel, 1997; 1999; Fulcher, 1998

[3] For a brief and relatively non-technical introduction to IRT see Baker, 1997. A much more detailed text is Crocker & Algina, 1986. For readers who wish to understand the statistics involved in IRT a useful introduction is provided by Henning, 1987

[4] A demo version of *FastTEST* can be downloaded from the ASC website at http://www.assess.com/FastTESTPro.html

[5] The Resources in Language Testing Page is available at http://www.surrey.ac.uk/ELI/ltr.html

[6] Sylvan Psychometric is contracted by ETS to deliver the TOEFL CBT worldwide. Their services and operations are described on their web page at http://www.sylvan prometric.com/

[7] DIALANG is an acronym for Diagnostic Language Assessment Details of the DIALANG project are available from the project website at http://www.jyu.fi/DIALANG/

[8] *PhonePass*™ is the trade mark of the computerised speaking test produced by Ordinate INC. Details of Ordinate products and services is available from its web site at http://www.ordinate.com/index.html. Visitors may arrange to take a sample test over the Internet

[9] Full-text research papers on e-rater are made available by ETS at http://www.ets.org/research/erater.html

Bibliography

AERA APA NCME (1999) *Standards for Educational and Psychological Testing*: Washington DC: American Educational Research Association, American Psychological Association, National Council on Measurement in Education

Alderson J C (1988) Innovations in Language Testing: Can the Microcomputer Help?: *Special Report No 1 Language Testing Update* University of Lancaster

Alderson J C (In press) Technology in Testing: The present and the future in Fulcher G (Ed.) *Expanding perspectives on language testing in the 21st century* Special Edition of System on Language Testing *System 28*

APA (1986) *Guidelines for Computer Based Tests and Interpretations*: American Psychological Association

Baker R (1997) Classical Test Theory and Item Response Theory in Test Analysis: *Special Report No 2: Language Testing Update* University of Lancaster

Barnwell D (1996) *A History of Foreign Language Testing in the United States* Arizona Bilingual Press

Bernstein J (1997) Speech Recognition in Language Testing. In Huhta A, V Kohonen, L Lurki-Suonio & S Luoma (Eds.) *Current Developments and Alternatives in Language Assessment* Jyvaskyla University

Bernstein J (1998) *Construct Comparison between the Language Proficiency Interview (LPI) and the PhonePass™ Test* Available on-line at http://www.ordinate.com/pdf/ConstructComparisonLPI990826.pdf

Bernstein J (1999a) *PhonePass™ Testing: Structure and Construct* Available on-line at http://www.ordinate.com/pdf/StructureAndConstruct990826.pdf

Bernstein J (1999b) *PhonePass™ Data Analysis: Correspondence with Oral Interviews and First-Language Bias Analysis* Available on-line at: http://www.ordinate.com/pdf/StructureAndConstruct990826.pdf

Brown J D (1997) Computers in Language Testing: Present research and some future directions *Language Learning & Technology 1 1* Available on-line at http://polyglot.cal.msu.edu/llt/vol1num1/brown/default.html

Bunderson C V, D I Inouye & J B Olsen (1989) The four generations of computerized educational measurement. In Linn R L (Ed.) *Educational Measurement (3rd edition)* American Council on Education

Burstein Jill & Martin Chodorow (1999) Automated Essay Scoring for Nonnative English Speakers *Joint Symposium of the Association of Computational Linguistics and the International Association of Language Learning Technologies Workshop on Computer-Mediated Language Assessment and Evaluation of Natural Language Processing College Park* June 1999 Available on-line at http://www.ets.org/research/acl99rev.pdf

Burstein J, L T Frase, A Ginther & L Grant (1996) Technologies for Language Assessment *Annual Review of Applied Linguistics 16*

Burstein J (1997) Scoring Rubrics: Using Linguistic Description to Automatically Score Free-Responses. In Huhta A, V Kohonen, L Lurki-Suonio & S Luoma (Eds.) *Current Developments and Alternatives in Language Assessment* Finland Jyvaskyla University

Chalhoub-Deville M (1999) (Ed.) *Issues in computer adaptive testing of reading proficiency Issues in Language Testing Vol 10* Cambridge University Press

Chalhoub-Deville M Alcaya C & Lozier V M (1997) *Language and Measurement Issues in Developing Computer-Adaptive Tests of Reading Ability: The Minnesota Approach.* In Huhta A, V Kohonen, L Lurki-Suonio & S Luoma (Eds.) *Current Developments and Alternatives in Language Assessment* Jyvaskyla University

Chalhoub-Deville & Deville C (1999) Computer adaptive testing in second language contexts *Annual Review of Applied Linguistics 19*

Crocker L & J Algina (1986) *Introduction to Classical and Modern Test Theory* Holt Rinehart & Winston

Davidson F (in press) The Language Tester's Statistical Toolbox in Fulcher G (Ed.) *Expanding perspectives on language testing in the 21st century* Special Edition of System on Language Testing *System 28*

Douglas D (2000) *Assessing Languages for Specific Purposes* Cambridge University Press

Dunkel P A (1997) Computer-Adaptive Testing of Listening Comprehension: A Blueprint for CAT Development. *The Language Teacher Online 21 10* Available on-line at http://langue.hyper.chubu.ac.jp/jalt/pub/tlt/97/oct/dunkel.html

Dunkel P A (1999) Considerations in developing or using second/foreign language proficiency computer-adaptive tests. *Language Learning & Technology 2 2* 77–93. Available on-line at http://polyglot.cal.msu.edu/llt/vol2num2/article4/index.html

Edgeworth F Y (1888) The statistics of examinations *Journal of the Royal Statistical Society 51*

Edgeworth F Y (1890) The element of chance in competitive examinations *Journal of the Royal Statistical Society 53*

Eignor D, C Taylor, I Kirsche & J Jamieson (1998) Development of a Scale for Assessing the Level of Computer Familiarity of TOEFL Examinees. *TOEFL Research Report 60* Princeton NJ: Educational Testing Service. Available on-line at ftp://etsis1.ets.org/pub/toefl/275756.pdf

ETS (1998) *Computer-based TOEFL score user guide* Educational Testing Service

Frase L T (1997) Technology for Language Assessment and Learning: Introduction and comments on the State of the Art. In Huhta A, V Kohonen, L Lurki-Suonio & S Luoma (Eds.) *Current Developments and Alternatives in Language Assessment* Jyvaskyla University

Freedle R (1990) *Artificial Intelligence and the Future of Testing* Lawrence Erlbaum

Fulcher G (1996) Does thick description lead to smart tests? A data-based approach to rating scale development *Language Testing 13 2*

Fulcher G (1998) Computer based language testing: The call of the internet. In Coombe A (Ed.) *Current Trends in English Language Testing Vol 1 Conference Proceedings for CTELT 1997 and 1998* Al Ain United Arab Emirates TESOL Arabia

Fulcher G (1999) Computerizing an English Language Placement Test *English Language Teaching Journal 53 4*

Fulcher G (In press) Review of Chalhoub-Deville M 1999 (Ed.) *Issues in computer adaptive testing of reading proficiency*: Issues in Language Testing Vol 10 Cambridge University Press *Language Testing 17 2*

Fulcher G & Thrasher R *Video FAQs: Introducing Topics in Language Testing* ILTA [online] available: http://www.surrey.ac.uk/ELI/ilta/faqs/main.html

Ginther A & Chawla A (1997) Multimedia – Words with Pictures: Unpacking the Effects of Visual Accompaniments to Listening Comprehension Items. In Huhta A, V Kohonen, L Lurki-Suonio & S Luoma (Eds.) *Current Developments and Alternatives in Language Assessment* Jyvaskyla University

Gruba P & C Corbel (1998) Computer-based testing in Clapham C & Corson D (Eds.) Language Testing and Assessment Vol 7 *Encyclopedia of Language and Education* Dordrecht: Kluwer Academic Publishers

Henning G (1987) *A Guide to Language Testing: Development evaluation research* Newbury House

Holtzman W H (Ed.) (1970) *Computer-assisted instruction testing and guidance* Harper Row

Kirsch I, J Jamieson, C Taylor & D Eignor (1998) Computer Familiarity Among TOEFL Examinees *TOEFL Research Report 59* Educational Testing Service. Available on-line at ftp://etsis1.ets.org/pub/toefl/275755.pdf

Lado R (1961) *Language Testing* Longman

Larsen-Freeman D & M Long (1991) *An Introduction to Second Language Acquisition Research* Longman

Messick S (1989) Validity. In Linn R L *Educational Measurement* American Council on Education/Macmillan 1

Perkins K, S R Brutten & S M Gass (1996) An investigation of patterns of discontinuous learning: Implications for ESL measurement *Language Testing 13 1*

Robinson P & S Ross (1996) The Development of Task-Based Assessment in English for Academic Purposes Programs *Applied Linguistics 17 4*

Spearman C (1907) Demonstration of formulae for true measurement of correlation *American Journal of Psychology 18*

Spearman C (1913) Correlations of sums and differences *British Journal of Psychology 5*

Sperling D (1998) *The Internet Guide for English Language Teachers* Prentice Hall

Spolsky B (1995) *Measured Words* Oxford University Press

Taylor C, J Jamieson, D Eignor & I Kirsch (1998) *The Relationship between Computer Familiarity and Performance on Computer-based TOEFL Test Tasks TOEFL Research Reports 61* Princeton NJ Educational Testing Service. Available on-line ftp://etsis1.ets.org/pub/toefl/275757.pdf

Taylor C, I Kirsch, D Eignor & J Jamieson (1999) Examining the Relationship Between Computer Familiarity and Performance on Computer-based Language Tasks *Language Learning 49 2*

Thorndike E L (1904) *An Introduction to the Theory of Mental and Social Measurements* Science Press

Wood B D (1927) *New York experiments with new-type modern language tests* Macmillan